ADVANCE COPY

THE
BUSINESS
OF
IMAGE

The masculine pronoun has been used throughout this book.
This stems from a desire to avoid ugly and cumbersome language,
and no discrimination, prejudice or bias is intended.

First printed in 1991.

Kogan Page Limited
120 Pentonville Road
London N1 9JN

British Library Cataloguing in Publication Data

A CIP record for this book is available from the British Library.

ISBN 0 7494 0557 0

Designed and typeset by The Jenkins Group
Printed and bound in Great Britain by Riddles Ltd, Guildford and Kings Lynn.

The Business of Image

VISUALISING THE CORPORATE MESSAGE

BY NICHOLAS JENKINS

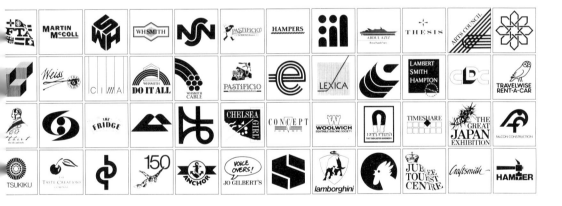

KOGAN PAGE

Contents

Introduction

Corporate: ... forming one body of many individuals.

Identity: ... condition or fact that a person or thing is itself and not something else; individuality, personality.

Oxford Dictionary

Stone age Palaeolithic rock painting. Symbolic femininity surpassing many contemporary attempts at simplified visual expression.

That every corporate body has some tangible identity is perhaps to state the obvious. However, the precise nature of its attitudes, aspirations, personality and function is not always apparent to the outside world or, in many cases, to the organisation itself. The act of creating a visual identity for an organisation not only focuses perceptions by defining, clarifying and communicating what is often a somewhat amorphous set of cultural components, but also acts as a management tool; consolidating internal morale, speaking with clarity to the market place, and carving out a competitive individuality.

The reasons why a company should embark on a corporate identity review can be legion and will depend upon specific circumstances, many of which I shall deal with later in this book, but there is no doubt that the results of such an exercise, if handled correctly, can only react positively on management, staff and customers alike.

There are many misconceptions surrounding the discipline - the perceived astronomic costs, the disagreeable notion of a designer telling a company how to run its business, the imposition of the ubiquitous logo on everything in sight being seen as the answer to the problem, or the feeling that the whole exercise is geared exclusively to multinational corporations. These are some of the myths I wish to explode by dealing with low-budget projects, client/consultant relationships, the totality of visual identity components and small to medium-sized company case histories.

Recent developments in corporate identity design have suggested that a panoply of experts in fields such as behaviourial and perception psychology are an essential adjunct to the process. While there is no doubt that such disciplines can contribute to the analysis of fundamental business management problems, it is my view that a successful and compelling visual identity is the product of the talent and experience of the designer and his understanding and relationship with his client. I have therefore devoted space to the nature of design itself in addition to its specific relationship to corporate requirements.

Fear, an inevitable component of our psyche, needs to be counteracted if we are to remain sane. The Egyptian magic eye, a symbol about which a designer today might be justifiably satisfied, is calculated to ward off evil and afford a degree of comfort and protection.

Having been a practitioner in the field since the early 1970s, I have been involved in a wide variety of projects ranging from major retail chains to small law practices, from trade unions to banks, and it is my intention in this book to explain the processes and management of a planned visual identity programme drawing on experience gained from as broad a spectrum as possible.

I make no apologies for the fact that the majority of case histories which I have used to illustrate various aspects of contemporary corporate identity design are projects with which I have been personally involved. I take the view that intimate practical knowledge is of more value than hypothesis.

Aztec hieroglyphics - mid-way between writing and symbolism - present an interesting conundrum to decipher, as their communication value depended more upon the cultural mores of the society in which they were produced than in their depiction of specific phenomena.

1   The Design Factor

It is doubtful whether some of the companies which are today household names would have been as successful as they are were it not for the careful design and control of their visible identities. Their reputations - the way in which they are regarded by their customers and staff - are largely the result of how they are perceived through the visual manifestations of their businesses; Shell projects a cheerful but solid reliability, IBM declares its technological superiority, British Airways reflects its newfound reliability and service.

The Greek Triskelion, symbolising victory and progress. Complex cultural ideas expressed in graphic form have more durability than the spoken word and are often the bricks from which a society is constructed.

Conversely, incredible mistakes have been made in the manipulation of perceived identities; the car marque MG, once a specific and totally understood image was devalued to the point of superficial anonymity by the notion of attaching its caché to mundane products in the hope that it would somehow create 'added value'; the end result was that the product devalued the identity.

The privatisation of parts of the London Transport bus system has resulted in total confusion; the 'big red bus' image - once an unmistakable symbol of a

The visible exteriorisation of a collective culture, manifestly proclaiming allegiance while sheltering in the security of belonging.

unique and localised transport system has been dissipated by a bewildering variety of vehicles, liveried in the various operators' individual graphic schemes; is it a bus? a coach? a sightseeing tour? Certainly not a super system, integrated and geared to the convenience and comprehension of its customers.

On the positive side, many organisations from every sector have managed to *reverse* decline by means of visual presentation. British Airways, the Prudential, British Home Stores, the Burton Group; all have experienced a renaissance in the late 1980s largely due to re-presentation; the subsequent economic recession would in all probability have crushed these icons of British commerce if their corporate and visual identities had not at the time been positively addressed.

It is, however, the medium and small organisations for whom a corporate identity programme is not infrequently the crucial ingredient which contributes to success. In a highly competitive business world, such programmes can prove to be deciding factors - the edge to which the market's perceptions can respond when faced with choice.

Identity design makes tangible what may be only latent and obscured; it lends individuality and character, it targets markets and elicits response, but the very nature of identity needs to be understood if it can be successfully communicated.

COLLECTIVE IDENTITY

Collective identity is a phenomenon which reflects a basic human need. The tribal instinct is in all of us and the exteriorisation of this psychology is something which has formed a large and tangible part of every recorded culture. Sometimes these visible identities have evolved as in African tribal body painting or the city business man's uniform, and sometimes they have been imposed, as in the case of IBM or Hitler's Third Reich. It is the latter - the consciously constructed visible face of an organisation or group which now concerns the increasing band of 'experts' in the field, but it is the former - the culturally evolved facets of any given society - which provide the visual language with which these programmes can be assembled.

Non-designer groups are extremely adept at creating and adhering to the exteriorisation of their particular corporate cultures. You can tell a public school boy a mile off as you can an adman, a construction worker or a bank clerk. Green wellies say different things about their owners than black wellies, as do cloth caps and bowlers, Volvos and Marinas. This is largely because people want to belong to groups, which is not always the case with a large corporation - by definition made up of a pyramidal structure of disparate (and unequal) personalities.

Corporate culture is largely about the way people behave, not the badge in their lapels; however, visual coherence is obviously one way in which people can

Cattle brands created by the Conquistadors in the sixteenth century. The Spanish in Mexico and Peru had a passion for imposing family symbols on everything they owned. This practice later translated itself into a kind of Wild West heraldry. Interestingly, this particular sequence of marks suggests the evolution of a Greek letter form.

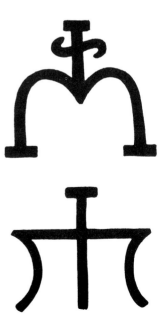

readily identify with each other and project their aspirations, and visual devices have been employed for this purpose since prehistory.

EVOLUTION OF VISUAL SYMBOLISM

The significance of the abstract graphic devices which intertwine the highly representational neolithic cave paintings in Africa and Europe have only very recently been understood - if still somewhat dimly.

It is thought that they represent visions produced by the nervous system when in a state of trance.

This phenomenon, when taken in conjunction with the apparent transformation of the depicted beasts into elongated human forms implies a powerful religious symbolism.

Religions have always been steeped in symbolism - some would say idolatry - but focus and coherence is achieved in a way which would be impossible without these visual manifestations of ideas.
The Assyrian god of war, Ashur, lacks no ambiguity of intent.

It takes sophisticated anthropological and archaeological detective work to arrive at this conclusion - our own generation has hitherto responded only to the aesthetic qualities of these works (considerable though they are) and missed entirely the purpose and meaning of the imagery. A different age - a different culture.

Hieroglyphics, pictograms and, later, what we now know as alphabets have to some extent removed the necessity for such highly symbolic and idiosyncratic visual treatments of essential cultural messages. More detail and depth can be ascribed to a subject if what we now understand as literacy is introduced into a culture (albeit until recently a facility available only to the top echelons of society).

The use of graphic symbolism therefore evolved into a mark of ownership rather than a means of cultural communication. In Greek excavations, potters' marks have been found on artifacts estimated to be 4,000 years old. As international trade expanded in Southern Europe during the fourth century BC, the need to denote ownership and origin increased.

By the Middle Ages, the use of merchants' marks was commonplace. In the fifteenth century publishers' imprints, guild marks and family emblems were an established part of the visual fabric of society. They were, however, only decipherable by the culture for which they were intended. The roots of oriental visual expression, for example, would have seriously inhibited the ability of the Japanese to distinguish one European mark from another.

In Japan, the development of graphic symbolism post-dated that of the West, probably because sino-script is in itself pictogrammatic. However, it is reasonable to suppose that the crests adopted by the aristocracy and the Samurai in the thirteenth century, allied to Western commercial influence, formed the basis for the eventual widespread use of commercial graphic symbolism in the East.

Three interpretations of deity emanating from different cultures; Shinto, Peruvian/Inca and North American Indian. Perhaps more visually emotive than a cross, but only if in ignorance of the act performed upon it. Cultural significance lends inestimable potency to symbolism.

The merchant, the painter and the potter have, from the middle ages onwards, proclaimed their function and their individuality through the use of personal emblems - the precursors of contemporary visual identity devices - though in many instances more expressive than their modern counterparts.

Heraldry is a complicated and perhaps irrelevant science in the context of today's corporate identity projections. However, in many respects it formed the basis of the idea in both Western and Eastern cultures that groups of individuals (in this case families) could be bonded together by lions, eagles and bears as a means of visual symbolism. Modern reinterpretations of heraldic devices are by no means uncommon, but still suffer from the fact that a lion is a lion - why not a tiger?

Traditional (royal) coat of arms.

Lion abstracted from a coat of arms to form a crest.

Modern interpretation of a heraldic lion for a machinery manufacturer.

Heraldry

Western heraldry, a vernacular much used (and mis-used) in visual identification, has its origins in practicality. Knights on medieval battlefields, totally encased in armour were, without identification, indistinguishable one from the other; the personal emblems placed on top of their helmets heralded their identity as well as helping to ward off blows to the head - these devices were known as crests.

During the eleventh and twelvth century crusades in the Middle East, the heat inside a suit of armour must have bordered on the unbearable and a surcoat of material often decorated with ferocious beasts was worn in order to reduce the inside temperature. The beasts were partly to frighten the enemy, but perhaps more importantly were a development of personal identity. The surcoats became known as Coats of Arms. The emblazoned devices found their way on to banners and flags; battle cries became mottoes and heraldry was born.

In the calmer times of the fourteenth and fifteenth centuries, this form of family identity became highly complex with various different devices being added through marriage; some kind of control became a necessity and a college of arms was founded in 1484 in order to contain the situation, an institution which, unbelievably, still exists today and in some respects competes with design consultants in creating visual identities.

Response

From the Roman potter's mark to the American West's cattle branding; from the medieval guild to the modern corporation; from the family coat of arms to the national flag, civilisations are drenched in graphic symbolism.

Japanese family crest.

Not surprisingly, some of the most powerful devices have been concerned with military aggression - though this in part is due to psychological association. The Roman, German, Austrian and American eagles (no coincidence here), the British lion or the Russian bear elicit diametrically opposed responses depending on from which perspective they are viewed.

The swastika commanded hatred from some (and still does) and respect and loyalty from others (and still, incredibly, does). In most liberal Western eyes, the symbol's uncompromising and aggressive angularity precisely matches what it has come to represent.

The Japanese sun flag, simple and direct in the extreme, cannot have engendered much respect at Pearl Harbour, but nevertheless remains a national symbol.

The Roman eagle, carried on high by resplendent legionnaires, must have been a daunting sight indeed. But it is the company, the corporation, which now has the wherewithal and more significantly the desire to identify itself - to proclaim its personality as the

Lions, eagles, bears; the stuff on which nations have been built.

nineteenth entury English aristocracy wished to do with their heraldry. They wore their badges on their sleeves as did the armies of the Third Reich - to express their purpose, their meaning and their culture, as did the neolithic cave dwellers.

CONTEMPORARY IDENTITY

Probably the most sophisticated, well managed and influential corporate identity to have been mounted in this century was the Adolf Hitler/Albert Speer scheme for the Third Reich. The combination of elements - the swastika, the black/white red shapes - and above all the juxtaposition and control with which these elements were used all combined to produce an aggressive and emotive ambience without the use of a single word or letter.

It was a highly innovative exercise, setting standards of implementation control which have been followed by most post-war multinational corporations. The ubiquitous design manual was born - a kind of design bible setting out in minute detail how every visual element is to be applied in any given situation. Talented designers were employed and centrally controlled, paradoxically much influenced by the Weimar Republic's Bauhaus designers, most of whom fled to the United States on the establishment of the Third Reich. A new controlled visual language was established with an efficiency and efficacy to which many contemporary organisations aspire and would be

Consistency of application and control combined with the use of powerful graphic elements introduced the twentieth century to the potential of a sophisticated corporate identity programme.

Computers are as good (or as bad) as their manipulators, and if allowed to dictate their own style and image parameters, will in a short space of time deaden their output. The Jean Machine device is the result of bending the computer's own rules in the direction of the designer's intention. 'Computerism' is still inherent in the result, but it remains an individual and apposite visual statement.

One of the most imaginative and, at the time, daring visual identity programmes. A boring old anti-social building company suddenly transformed into sweetness and light - one almost believes in the quality of life.
Designed by Wolff Olins.

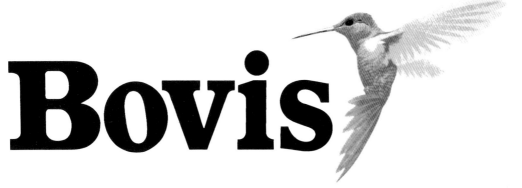

A Miro symbol for the Spanish
Tourist Office; an attempt to
humanise, through the language
of fine art, the new heraldry.
People respond more readily to
images which evoke an emotional
response rather than having to
solve an intellectual conundrum.

Another Miroesque attempt at
humanising an institution -
designed by Landor Associates -
in this case a bank. Perhaps more
of this fine art approach will
eventually permeate through into
the realisation that people
respond to images in the first
instance on an emotional level.
People are not computers; they
either like, dislike or are
indifferent. It is the indifference
which is the negative, and many
unfelt or intellectualised visual
messages can produce just that.

An American corporate identity
image circa 1920 - a superb
example of the genre in the
tradition of Toulouse-Lautrec as
poster artist. Corporate identity
designers (though not known by
that description at the time) were
by and large 'commercial artists'
- a derogatory term since the
1960s but valued by their
contemporaries in the higher
echelons of the profession. Art
and commerce - a Renaissance
melange.

justified in feeling a degree of envy.

However, this was essentially a domestic exercise. If the whole enterprise had succeeded and world domination had been achieved, there would have been considerable confusion in parts of India and Persia where the swastika is used as a religious or good luck symbol ... the kind of cultural *faux pas* it is perhaps difficult to guard against, but one which increasingly needs to be considered in the international context.

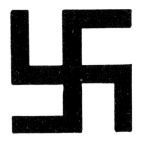

Oriental mystic symbol with connotations somewhat different from those intended due to events beyond the control of its adherents. The importance of context cannot be overrated.

After the war, the Harvard Business School was largely instrumental in persuading the future captains of industry that a controlled and considered visual identity was as essential a part of the corporate mix as quality control or marketing effort, and those corporations which embraced this notion reaped huge benefits at the expense of their competitors. IBM, Olivetti and Shell, to name a few, all became leaders in their fields.

INTERNATIONALISM
As the multinational organisation becomes more commonplace, one of the problems that will increasingly concern the designer in this field is how to communicate across a whole raft of cultural backgrounds. IBM will only be understood in China by repeated exposure, rather in the way that a no-parking sign, which has little visual logic, is understood only by its insistent presence.

Without massive and expensive exposure, a graphic device composed from the Roman alphabet would be unlikely to be understood or even responded to on an emotional level by societies exclusively nurtured on a pictogrammic culture. Likewise, Western response to Japanese devices is limited to the fact that they are evidently Japanese.

Traffic control symbols are often totally devoid of logic or pictorial cogency, yet generally speaking obeyed; the 'No Goods Vehicle' sign, even if encircled in red, could easily be taken as an invitation to proceed. Comprehension depends upon insistent exposure and the context in which they are employed.

An alarming lack of visual logic permeates many statutory devices which control our lives. The notion that a hexagon or an inverted triangle are somehow prohibitive is clearly bizarre. It is only because we have to learn these conventions that they are understood at all which largely diminishes the function of symbolism. In a corporate identity sense, this kind of confusion would be unacceptable.

This cultural bending can be an expensive business and requires extremely sophisticated manipulation across a broad media range if the specific qualities of an organisation are to become synonymous with, say, three letters from the Roman alphabet in an environment which writes and speaks only Cantonese. Likewise the meaning of a mark based on Japanese calligraphy would be opaque to Western eyes, however aesthetically interesting it may appear.

The quest for a kind of esperanto of design is both pressing and daunting - daunting in the sense that attempts to establish a common spoken word have so abjectly failed.

It may be that communication technology will dictate the form of visual identities while the common aspirations of the global business community will dictate the context. A computer generated dollar sign, when accessed on what will probably become our sole source of visual communication - the VDU - will say the same thing in the same way to all concerned - a dismal and, as with esperanto, a soulless prospect. A visual statement, if it is to communicate in any meaningful way, must elicit both intellectual and emotional responses. In truly international terms, these requirements are not often fulfilled.

Cultural Response

In a recent survey into the best-known brand names, the logotypes depicting the first three in the UK are

20

all remarkably similar in so far as they all employ a derivative of handwriting (St Michael, Cadbury, Kellogg's) while in Europe the first three are all circular devices (Mercedes-Benz, Philips and Volkswagen). This may well imply a cultural divergence on a relatively domestic scale; the island race responding to the expression of individuality and personalisation while in Europe a more global and all-embracing view is taken.

Anglo Saxon insularity as expressed by personal handwriting as opposed to the more global European view. These six devices all featured as the best-known brands in Europe and the UK in a recent survey.

Throughout history, very few truly universally understood symbolic devices have emerged. Those that have more often than not have done so for reasons other than their intrinsic communicative value. The Christian cross or the Star of David depend for its recognition on exposure and for a comprehension and understanding of the history and culture to which it belongs.

Shell petrol, employing as it does the direct link of illustrating its name, stands a good chance of intellectual recognition - but only in the vernacular of the English language. Likewise the Bell Telephone Company (now replaced by AT&T), but this does have the added dimension of depicting, if somewhat obliquely, its function. Perhaps one of the more succinct and universally comprehensible symbols devised during this century is the BOAC mechanised bird, but it lacks soul.

A telephone is a telephone, but a bell, designed by Saul Bass, (for the Bell Telephone Corporation) although oblique, adds a certain mental sonority which ensures memorability.

The three religions of which the West is most aware.
The significance of the symbology has been superseded by familiarity through exposure.

BOAC's somewhat sterile mechanistic bird device was nonetheless an example of the use of a universal visual language - not dependent on cultural esotericism for the communication of its function.

International information pictograms, largely developed by a series of Olympic Games committees are on the whole successful in communication terms, but are not obliged to express personality or elicit emotional response. A telephone is, after all, a telephone.

In the context of the latter part of the twentieth century, with the astonishing growth of information technology and the need to create global markets, the problems inherent in creating the international identity which will communicate across cultural and language barriers are not easily resolved; the visual components need by definition to possess common denominators - *clichés*, even - but visually manipulated in such a way as to inject an individuality, character and ethos appropriate to their owner.

Received cultural signals need to be circumvented; a dog is a pet to some, a meal to others; a star means many things to many people and in certain forms, to certain people, spells anathema. Colour can be misconstrued - red can be a rag to a bull if politically interpreted; green can express ecological responsibility, but to Western superstition it means bad luck; funeral dress is decreed as either black or white according to which sector of the globe death occurs. These paradoxes can mean a minefield of potentially damaged sensibilities.

However, by obsessionally avoiding negatives, creative and effective solutions will be reduced to banality. The crucial attributes to which the aspiring international designer now needs to address himself are a knowledge of global cultural moeurs (historical and contemporary, sociological and political) and the vision and nerve to create a new visual language for corporate identification which does not rely on the narrow conventions established by the West in the early part of the twentieth century.

Globally there is a danger that corporate identity solutions will be watered down to their lowest common denominator - desperately trying to avoid misinterpretation by disparate and often contradictory cultures. The six pointed star is not good news in Arab countries, WH Smith is unpronounceable in France, and the Americans are unlikely to respond positively to an Iraqi acronym.

Cultural Shifts
Although it appears at the moment that no truly original approaches to design are surfacing, there have from time to time been sudden traumatic cultural shifts which have swept away received and expected images and created entirely new visual vernaculars.

Mao had his cultural revolution, as for that matter did Hitler, though both were mercifully short-lived in terms of changing our political aspirations. Gentler revolutions have occurred in the purely visual field:

The Olympic Games have provided lush pastures for the graphic designer - the identity and all its concomitant appendages being studiously re-designed for each occasion. Perhaps one day we shall arrive at a universal and immutable visual language for such things.

the Impressionists, the pre-Raphaelites and abstract art have all significantly shifted our visual perceptions, but in terms of design the pre-war Bauhaus and the seventies Pop Movement were the last significantly new visions that we have experienced in this century.

Businesses are predominantly the designer's clients, and risks are expensive luxuries - but it is only by taking risks that any Bauhaus or Pop-type revolution in design vernaculars can come about. If we are to cease fiddling with the expected and create new visual languages it will take the collective talent of the Impressionists allied to the courageous and risk-taking patronage of industry if new ground is to be broken.

A NEW PERSPECTIVE?

Corporate design on any scale needs to considerably enlarge its vocabulary if the borders of visual communication are to be crossed effectively. If there is such a thing as a collective culture, it must surely be embedded in human emotions and the only truly global language used to express these elusive facets of the human condition is Art. Intellectual analysis is crucial to understanding a problem but to solve that problem in visual terms requires the elucidation of an emotional response. Companies consist of people, not as yet computers, and corporations speak to other people, not as yet automatons. The swastika now produces feelings of revulsion because of what it came to represent while the Bovis hummingbird suggests

A Bauhaus prospectus designed by Laszlo Moholy-Nagy in 1924 - a graphic approach which has strongly influenced corporate graphics in the 1980s in the search for 'something new'.

24

benevolent activity. The banality of Shell's shell is only alleviated by the way in which it is drawn - producing a comfortable and stable image; on the other hand, it is difficult to muster much good feeling for a company which represents itself with its initial letters tortured into a monogram - the kind of 'new heraldry' much favoured in the 1960s.

There are signs that a more emotionally based response to visual identity is beginning to surface. Juan Miro, the Spanish painter, in addition to creating the Spanish tourist symbol, was also commissioned to produce a tapestry to hang in the main foyer of a Catalonian bank. He was required to express the artistic heritage of Catalonia and to project the social responsibility of La Caixa. The design consultants Landor suggested abstracting a section of this work to form the central visual device around which to build the bank's identity. The result is a statement calculated to elicit a human response, not a set of intellectual conundrums, and therefore has the potential of operating on a multicultural level.

Searching the past for pastiche and perhaps fashionable solutions can be a sterile exercise if the original is better than its derivative. German typography of the 1930s, although often mimicked in the 1980s in the interests of 'new directions', possesses fundamental tenets which remain intact in their own right and it is an unworthy ploy to purloin their standards in the interests of creating some 'new' visual statement in the interests of ephemeral novelty.

PERCEPTIONS

When considering visual components geared to expressing an identity, it is worth noting that most visual stimuli are by necessity conservative, not to say conventional, if in our current climate they are to be readily understood by their target audience. Motor cars, for example, have not radically changed their appearance from the horseless carriage which was their antecedent, partly because people expect them to appear as they do (though with fashion oriented appendages in order to denote their newness) and partly because the technology has not changed in any fundamental way. Newspapers are immediately recognisable for what they are, their design carefully reflecting their specific markets.

The Times editorial approach, if treated visually in the style of The *Sun* would be too shocking to contemplate, and vice versa. To compound the problem, our preconceptions of how things should appear are often anachronistic; ocean liners have funnels (in fact they are style statements which conceal air conditioning vents) and business men wear bowler hats (actually nowadays they rarely do).

The fact that people perceive things in the way they think they *ought* to look can be turned to advantage if used in an original and interesting way, a phenomenon often exploited by designers.

THE BALANCE

Given any scale of project, from a multinational to a one man band, successful visual interpretation of a corporate identity depends on creative inspiration - but inspiration based on a total understanding of the nature and purpose of the exercise. Research and analysis are therefore crucial ingredients of the corporate identity process and are discussed in the next chapter. However, it is my contention that they are support mechanisms for the designer's inspiration, not an end in themselves.

Generally speaking we accept things for what they are and are disturbed by the unexpected or the unnatural. It is the skewing of normality which can produce a jolt to the sensibilities, compelling our attention and therefore our attention and therefore our response...an approach much used in fine art, but considered dangerous in commercial terms. Risks however are the things on which successes are built.

2   Creative Research

An identity scheme for a group of bakeries, calculated to present a unitied and cohesive image.

In the interests of underlining the new professionalism which has by necessity accompanied the design industry's recent and rapid growth, research has become regarded by many as a natural adjunct to the consultancy's offer, particularly in the field of corporate design. In-depth knowledge of a client's ethos, aspirations, markets, etc must undeniably be crucial in arriving at a relevant and well targeted design solution; however, there is a suspicion in some sections of the industry that emphasis on research, while contributing to the clients' perception of professionalism, does little to enhance the creative solution, the result of which is that there is a growing polarisation of attitude as to the relevance of this innovation. The line between business management and corporate identity consultancies has, over recent years, been drawn ever more finely.

In order to define an identity it is necessary to possess one. If no discernible culture or purpose exists, then it is evident that one must be created if a company is intent on exteriorising itself to its markets. Alternatively, a company may independently have formulated well defined innovative or evolutionary objectives but, unclear as to how these may be achieved, enlists the offices of exterior consultants.

There are management consultants who purport to offer corporate identity design and, in the belief that these two disciplines are inextricably intertwined in the creative process, there are corporate identity consultants who offer expertise in restructuring and positioning programmes. There can be no rules; every company is unique in its requirements and there is space for wide-ranging combinations of input.

At its simplest, consultancies tend either to be research led (the larger groups) or design led (the smaller groups whose facilities - and for that matter personalities - are generally not geared to producing an in-depth analysis of the nature of their clients and their markets prior to launching into creative solutions). There is no doubt that the 400- page report, if not entirely relevant, can stultify the creative mind, often resulting in visual solutions which are at best an attempt to synthesise a set of intellectual conclusions about the nature of the client, or at worst a kind of minimalised visual statement which will not rock any boats. The Eureka Syndrome on the other hand - the pure gut solution - can often fall short of the long-term requirements if insufficient study is made of the client's markets, his culture, or his aspirations.

A complicating and perhaps more serious factor which

straddles these two *modus operandi* is the fact that corporate identity solutions from whichever source are now rarely innovative. The new heraldry of the corporate symbol seems to have imposed its dead hand across the board.

In order for research to positively contribute to the creative visual solution and form the basis for innovation it must be tailor-made to that end. A business management audit can suggest that a corporate identity programme would significantly contribute to any proposed repositioning mix and as such does a favour to the design industry, but it is unlikely that it can contribute a great deal to the construction of a brief. Likewise, blanket and unstructured interviews with all and sundry will simply result in an unfocused and generalised profile from which the designer can draw almost any conclusion he wishes.

The designer requires specific information on which to base his conclusions, and this can be defined according to the nature of the client. On the basis of a two axis matrix, it is feasible to identify the type of information required and the key individuals from whom it can be obtained. For example, a scale can be constructed representing the extremities of competitiveness in the marketplace on the one hand and a non-competitive stance on the other (ie a mass market retail chain as opposed to a national institution). In order to extract the relevant information in each case, the bias of the data which needs to be assembled alters significantly.

An interrelated scale running from external sources (the competition, the consumer) to internal (those whose remit it is to create and maintain the culture of the organisation), will identify the individuals to be interviewed.

Gathered information is subject to subjectivity. Somehow it must be decided who the recipients of an inquisition in the interests of self knowledge should be. The tea lady should, if true democracy is to be exercised, be consulted.

On the other hand, if the tea lady does not care for the new culture about to be imposed on her environment, she has the freedom, at least in our society, to absent herself from the ensuing upheaval. Research into the culture and *raison d'être* of any organisation must be directed squarely at those who really matter to the strategic direction of the organisation. Research programmes calculated to arrive at conclusions which are relevant to the construction of a visual identity programme need to source information from specific areas. The more competitive an organisation is, the more external and objective the views need to be. Organisations in a less or non-competitive situation have the luxury of creating and expressing their own ethos without undue market pressure being brought to bear and internal sources are in this case more relevant.

INFORMATION SOURCES

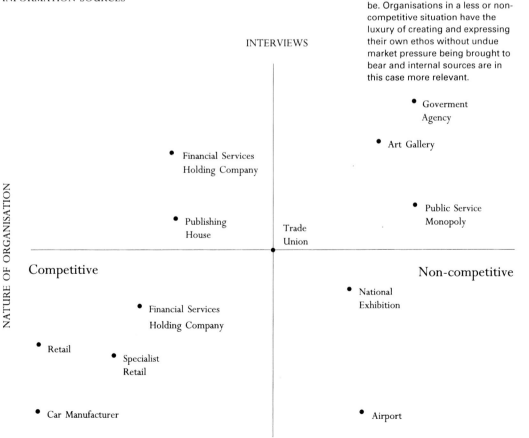

INTERVIEWS

- Goverment Agency
- Art Gallery
- Financial Services Holding Company
- Public Service Monopoly
- Publishing House

Trade Union

NATURE OF ORGANISATION

Competitive

Non-competitive

- National Exhibition
- Financial Services Holding Company
- Retail
- Specialist Retail
- Car Manufacturer
- Airport

In physical terms, a company consists of management, staff, product and environment. The subjective view of this melange will come from within, the objective view from competitors and customers. Research will balance these views according to their relevance; the designer (the third eye) can then make an informed assessment of the ethos of his client while not being diverted by extraneous management information.

SYNTHESIS = FOCUSED BRIEF

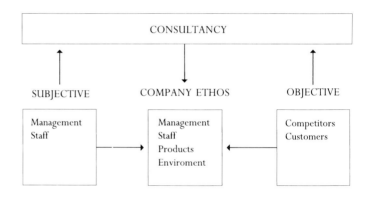

Balance of the objective and the subjective - perhaps the most problematic of all intellectual exercises related to the projection of a coherent culture. The outside voice requires attention and respect, while the inner culture yearns for preservation. One of the most valuable aspects of any external research, be it for whatever purpose, is the objectivity it brings to bear on problems which are often submerged in an existing culture. Equally, it is crucial for the design consultant to understand that culture, warts and all.

The attitudes of those within any organisation towards its own ethos will probably differ from those without - a synthesis of these opposing views, choosing those most relevant to the marketplace and discarding those which are negative will produce a cultural laundering from which a focused image can be produced.

Research of any kind will throw up plus and minus factors. The plus factors can simply be inculcated into the conclusion; however, the minus factors can either be ignored or presented in a better light (at the client's peril) or they can be re-filtered back through management for correction prior to inclusion in the brief. It is by this method that the client benefits in management terms from research basically tailored to the design brief.

32

MANAGEMENT BENEFIT SPIN OFF

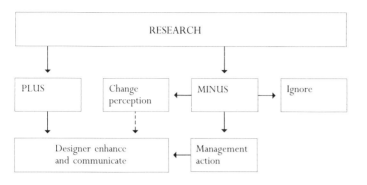

Information flow must be geared to complement and enhance the designer's inspiration. Corporate identity solutions have to produce emotional responses as well as intellectual communication.

Total perfection is an unlikely conclusion of any enquiry into an organisation's culture and aspirations. The opportunity for corrective action is therefore afforded by a research programme, even if specifically geared to the formulation of a visual identity. The options of disregarding or disguising warts is not recommended. No one cares for criticism, especially not from some long-haired designer. The corporate identity designer however cannot function without information on which to base his visual conclusions. On the path to understanding his client's persona, he will inevitably stumble across some unsavoury elements (at least as they appear to him). These can be reported, discussed, analysed, rejected, accepted or simply ignored. But it is the task of any communicator to ensure that the projection matches the reality.

It is the spark, the creative insight, the talent (albeit through received culture) which will determine whether or not the designer's visual expression of an organisation's relevance to its markets and its staff will actually ring bells. A structure must be established in order to enable this talent to work. The designer must be involved from day one - be part of the research process - in order to fully comprehend the ethos of the subject which he will eventually need to communicate.

If maximum benefit is to be gained from the talent and communication skills of the designer, he needs to understand the precise nature of his subject. Different perspectives need to be balanced one against the other - the objective and the subjective - as a catalyst for his imagination.

INFORMATION FLOW

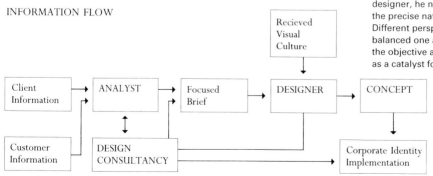

The 'quick sketch,' a device much used since this drawing of Prince Albert which represented the visual identity of an exhibition of his life and work in the early 1980s. Its impression of immediacy was not achieved as instantaneously as it might appear, it being a pasted up amalgam of several hours' worth of 'instant' pen and brush strokes. The difficulty was to achieve a balance between portraying the dignity of the subject while at the same time expressing a certain levity appropriate to a personage who was in fact less ponderous than he is often portrayed.

The Belfont Lake device, also employing a sketch technique, is counterpointed by a strict typographic form.

The Pentagram designed image for British Trade Weeks, circa 1961, a government promotional scheme held in various cities abroad. As with the Albert drawing being an early example of a genre since perhaps overused, this was one of the first successful examples of the Union Jack being employed in a contemporary visual idiom.

BRITAIN AT EXPO '92

Britain's World Fair image - a complex re-arrangement of elements of the Union Jack national flag - achieves its dynamic by breaking out of the constraints of its background. Official national images such as flags are inevitably clichés, but if manipulated in an original manner, the cliché becomes an advantage by instantly establishing, in this case, nationality.

BRITAIN

36

Obviously the degrees of research input will vary according to the size and complexity of the project. If, however, design consultancy research continues in its current vein it is possible that creativity, innovation and sheer joy will seep out of corporate design. It is the *focus* of the research that will free the designer to arrive at the most creative and compelling work.

CORPORATE CULTURE

A definition of an existing culture can only be achieved by objective research; positive adjustments to that known culture can only be achieved by innovative management decisions and these can in turn be reflected by visual corporate identity.

To discover the personality of an organisation is a highly complex affair; companies, as with people, are full of paradoxes, many of which management will be unaware. 'This is the way we do things around here' or 'we've always done it this way, why change?' are common resistant responses to enquiries into what makes a company what it is.

There are instances, particularly in small or medium-sized companies, when an unusually charismatic chief executive can mould the character of his organisation by making it an extension of himself. This can result in an idiosyncratic persona which will, for better or worse, create an individual and self-sustaining culture which may best be left alone. Most organisations however, are constructed from a myriad of components, all interacting one upon the other. Tradition, history and fierce loyalty to the founder's philosophy can create a bedrock on which to build or on the other hand simply serve to ossify the company, stultifying innovation.

Hierarchical structure, management style, communication systems, decision processes and recruitment methods all signal aspects of company culture. The care with which a company treats its clients and its employees (training, rewards, etc) will communicate a great deal about management attitudes. To research, define and synthesise these cultural elements is not a simple matter, and analysis requires great perspicacity and sensitivity.

Statistics are not unimportant in this kind of research; if it is discovered that 90 per cent of sales pitches are lost, something within the culture must surely be awry; if 50 per cent of employees leave after four months, something serious must be amiss with their working environment; if only 15 per cent of staff avail themselves of the staff canteen, it is too expensive, too uncongenial in its ambience or the food is lousy. These problems can be statistically identified, but cannot be resolved by visual identity alone; a company tie will not clinch a sale, logotypes woven into the carpet will not retain staff and new wallpaper in the canteen will not cover the essential cracks. Cultural research must be used as a basis for innovation and change - the management benefit spin-off - before it can be translated into a visual identity.

FOCUSING THE PERCEIVED PROBLEM

The General, Municipal, Boilermakers and Allied Trades Union GMBATU, on the accession of a new General Secretary, and in the light of changing attitudes to industrial relations generally, decided to modify its somewhat confrontational stance. By the late 1980s, all union membership had for some years been declining, partly due to the workforce generally perceiving the relevance of unions to their particular needs as being less than focused and the fact that Scargillism and the print unions' confrontation were seen to have been largely counterproductive. There was therefore (and still is) fierce competition amongst the unions for a share of a dwindling pool of membership.

A visual expression of the Trade Union GMBATU. Somewhat neo-Fascist in tone, despite the conjoining of hands. But whose hands? Certainly not the employer's.

The leadership decided to target a membership drive by widening the unions representational base by addressing an undertapped but increasing potential - women - and by increasing the number of 'products' and overall services available to the membership. The problem was that GMBATU did not appear in any way to reflect this new approach. Their slogan 'Unity is Strength', their colours - black and red - and their style of graphic presentation all combined to undermine the leadership's intended message. This dichotomy having been perceived, the proposition that if the new approach were to be more accurately reflected and effectively conveyed, a visual corporate identity programme would be an essential ingredient of the message.

Certain assumptions were made as to the willingness of members to accept a visual identity change, as opinion had already been canvassed by the union with positive reactions concerning the new, more caring and non-confrontational stance adopted by the leadership. If the reality of intention was deemed acceptable to the membership, it would seem reasonable to suppose that a visual expression of that intent would be embraced without any overt culture shock. However, union structure is unlike that of a commercial organisation in so far as the normal pyramidal structure associated with company management is to some extent inverted. Theoretically, union management's *raison d'être* is to carry out the will of the membership, and any suspicion of imposition from above might well impinge on traditional organisational values.

A research programme was therefore essential in order to verify the membership's compliance with the leadership's aspirations and to ascertain whether an expected radical change of presentational style would be acceptable without an approval committee of several million adjudicators.

A series of interviews was conducted in various demographic areas with union officials, shop stewards and shop floor members with surprisingly positive results, practically all interviewees being in tune with the leadership's thinking and displaying no dismay at the demise of traditional union banners. Furthermore, there was general contentment that the leadership should take responsibility for any repositioning identity programme.

The conclusions drawn from this exercise formed the basis for the design solutions; a softer more caring and less confrontational ethos was overwhelmingly required; a degree of humour would be a welcome change from the traditional austerity of trade union imagery and a more democratic flavour would more closely correspond to the membership's aspirations.

The solution consisted of a combination of factors:

1. GMBATU was changed to the more succinct GMB, the full name being dropped (the word 'boilermakers' is not only anachronistic, but has strong overtones of traditional working class - not an element thought to be relevant).

2. Two linked figures were 'grown' out of a logotype constructed from the GMB letters. These are deliberately counterpointed in style in order to 'lighten' the message, and represent male and female (though with a degree of ambiguity).

3. A strap line 'working together' was devised, and is visually always part of the logotype. This forms

A new attitude, a new social climate, a new relevance. 'Working together' is deliberately ambiguous. Ethnic minorities, women, employers, employees, government. Pragmatism triumphs over confrontation.

The balance between overt paternalism and genuine integration of ambitions is a delicate equation. Black and white photography (albeit by a much revered photographer - Don McCullum) is perceived to be cost conscious - a crucial factor in a union leader's credibility to his membership. On the other hand, a non-condescending approach to its presentation retains a dignity essential to the communication of the ambitions of the leadership.

a prefix for any given message; ie: 'working together for the health service'.

4. The colour combination is yellow and blue - soft but not over-feminine, politically neutral and high contrast in terms of legibility.

5. The overall typographic style is calculated to be responsible but not ponderous, legible but not dull.

6. High quality but simple black and white photography by Don McCullum is used throughout the publications, succinctly conveying the various messages without appearing to be expensive or frivolous.

The identity was launched at the 1987 annual conference to general acclaim. During the year following the launch, the GMB was the only union to have actually increased their membership (other than by mergers); an extra 4,000 members being attributable to the scheme and its marketing support material. The profile of the union has been considerably raised, not least by the extensive editorial given to the initiative.

The sense of 'belonging', a crucial factor in stemming what could have been a tide of defections, has been greatly enhanced. Female membership is increasing, as is the number of industries in which the GMB is operating. The vast improvement in corporate

PAY

CONDITIONS

HEALTH & SAFETY.

YOU'RE BUILDING THE FUTURE.

WE'RE WORKING FOR YOURS.

GMB
working together

in the building industry

nk ind

communications, both internal and external, has resulted in a more homogeneous and united organisation which is now transmitting the right messages in a more conciliatory (as opposed to confrontational) tone. The GMB's enhanced credibility has resulted in it being listened to and taken seriously by government, industry, the public and the trade union movement as a whole.

The corporate identity has accurately and forcefully translated the GMB's aspirations into reality, resulting in quantifiable and tangible results - a breakthrough in trade union philosophy.

The designer's requirements from research cannot be formularised. Due to the GMB's relatively limited resources, the information necessary for formulating a relevant and effective visual identity had to be prioritised, political acceptability being the prime consideration. However, in the case of a more market-orientated organisation, a broader spread of opinion would need to be canvassed. Recruitment, internal loyalty and cohesion certainly need to be addressed in any research geared to an identity programme, but in a purely commercial context the consumer/customer becomes the prime source of information.

3 The Management Decision

To embark upon a corporate identity programme is a decision not to be taken lightly; if the process is not conceived, structured and managed correctly, significant quantities of money and management time can easily be squandered. Business decisions are based on identified requirements; in the case of corporate identity, it is of paramount importance that these are focused and clearly defined before contemplating a move which can radically alter both internal and external perceptions, if not the entire nature of the business. Given the sophisticated techniques which have, over recent years, been developed in the field of identity design, perceptions can be manipulated in almost any direction but it is a dangerous notion to exploit this communication tool in order to paper over the cracks; to be 'found out' in the sense that the offer is seen to contradict reality can result in seriously negative reactions.

If no fundamental change is contemplated to the fabric or ethos of the company and all is well, it could be argued that to re-present it in more

An identity scheme for the International Hospitals Group, concerned with developing multi-ethnic hospital projects in the Middle East.

Marks and Spencer is and always has been a much revered institution, firmly embedded in the British way of life. Value, reliability, safeness, but in the context of the retail explosion of the early 1980s a trifle dull. To some, a snobbish joke; to others, a lifeline. Its graphic presentation was complacent, dated, quaint and, it must be said, ill considered.

relevant, coherent and focused terms is sufficient justification in itself; however, in order to accurately define a company in visual terms it is necessary to establish exactly what it is that the company represents. It is not infrequent for skeletons to tumble out of cupboards during this process - a spin-off opportunity for management action.

In any competitive environment, criteria for success are constantly shifting whether they be a company restructure, the opening up of new markets, acquisitions, mergers or, for that matter, the exterior influence of a stylistic shift in accepted visual language which outmodes an existing image. The management of change cannot easily be achieved without visual support. These developments can be communicated to advantage through an evolving visual identity or a radical repositioning exercise, depending upon the degree to which existing values are deemed advantageous.

FORCED DECISION

In the late 1970s Marks and Spencer, building on a period of unprecedented success, decided to expand both its estate in the UK and simultaneously establish itself in Europe. In addition, new merchandise areas were under consideration and some existing departments were to be expanded in response to growing consumer demand in, for example, the food and household furnishings sectors. Consumer research identified one central problem; that of in-store signing. A proportion of established customers were found to be unaware of new and unfamiliar product areas, while in multi-storey stores, the customer presence on the ground floor far exceeded that of departments on upper floors, even when departments were interchanged. Embarking upon solving this specific problem, it became evident that the visual components of the corporate identity did not fit comfortably into any ordered information or directional signing system.

The well-known 'St Michael' device was a crudely executed affair, arbitrarily imprisoned in a parallelogram; the type styles employed at the time were ponderous and dated and the corporate colour scheme lacked vibrance or a suitable degree of tonal contrast for easy legibility. These deficiencies were addressed in accordance with the in-store signing requirements but in so doing a fresher, more ordered and relevant corporate identity emerged which, over a period of a year, was applied to all visible aspects of the company; from stationery to vehicles, from garment labels to packaging.

A corporate identity by default, but one which required a management decision in the first place to instigate positive change in response to an identified need. The result was not radical - Marks and Spencer is an institution embedded in the British national psyche and it would have been imprudent to shift

The curious notion of St Michael being the brand name of Marks and Spencer is an established and accepted fact that it would have been dangerous to disturb. The visual elements which represented this relationship were, to say the least, both disparate and dated. No thought had been given to their application or visual synergy. An embedded love of a national institution was accepted, strategic marketing warts and all, but a visual rationalisation became an inevitable route to be pursued if the company was to retain its edge in an increasingly visually aware market-place.

consumers' perceptions in any overtly discernible direction.

MANAGEMENT AS DESIGNER

Marks and Spencer is an institution - and until recently apparently immutable. Its confidence in itself, its paternalism, could, in the 1970s, have been construed as arrogance. Their decision to export their particular brand of retailing expertise to the continent of Europe at that time was initially, if not disastrous, at least surprising for them in so far as the tenets established over many years in the UK were simply not appreciated by the Parisians or the Lyonnais. Much to the chagrin of the Marks and Spencer's directors, Watford High Street could not, it seemed, be profitably beamed down to the Boulevard Hausseman. Its identity, its *raison d'être* was only vaguely understood in Paris, and only then by people who had stumbled into the Marble Arch flagship store while on a weekend spree in London.

The idea, for example, of eschewing changing rooms in favour of immediate exchange of merchandise with no questions asked worked well in the UK, and still does, but it was an alien concept in Europe. M & S had created a specific culture for a specific market, and initially failed to grasp the fact that in order to export a culture it either has to be modified to suit its new environment or vast expenditure has to be authorised for an education programme involving the whole communications panoply of advertising, public relations and corporate identity.

To add insult to injury, the famous M&S green, one of the main ingredients of their UK identity, was banned for in-store promotional or signing use by the Paris Fire Department, it being the designated code colour for emergency exits. A new colour therefore had to be found which performed the same task - to provide a strong corporate colour statement while at the same time having sufficient tonal strength to support, as a background, the white and yellow/gold typography established in the UK which would be legible at considerable distances.

Yellow/gold is not an easy colour to satisfactorily relate to others; reds when combined are too sickly; blues are too 'cheap'; yellows, however orchestrated, lacking in contrast. Brown was decided upon, being capable of deep tonality and being aesthetically sympathetic with the secondary accent colour.

But which brown? On a tour around the UK flagship store and in the process of discussing the European problem *vis à vis* M&S's so far less than satisfactory entry into that market, a senior executive seized a pair of brown suede Hush Puppy shoes and holding them aloft established the exact corporate colour to be employed henceforth throughout Europe.

This is by no means a cynical criticism; rather an observation that the art/science of corporate identity has moved forward a considerable degree since the last decade. Senior management from almost any business sector would now be embarrassed by dictating corporate image by personal preference. However, in the event 'Hush Puppy brown' turned out to have been the right and inspired choice for a major expansion programme; luck triumphed over judgement, and a new graphic scheme was successfully introduced; changing rooms were installed and Watford High Street submerged into a degree of Gallic culture.

Today, there is no doubt that given the same set of circumstances, a different and more sophisticated approach would have been adopted; in another ten years' time, it is probable that visual identity decisions taken today will be regarded as uninformed and naive. We progress.

Europe in the late 1970s was to UK retailers a foreign field - it still to a large extent, remains so. The conundrum presented to the French of 'St Michael, le marque de Marks & Spencer' was not the only baffling component of its offer. 'You can't try on the clothes, bring them back if they don't fit' was a concept which was not initially understood. Compromise prevailed. M&S's subsequent success in Europe is due to a commendable bending of its corporate stance - Watford High Street no longer reigns on the Boulevard Hausseman.

NEW FREEDOMS

By contrast, companies are often, at the mercy of market forces, obliged to change direction and must be seen to so do. In recent times this is particularly true of the now deregulated professions such as law and accountancy, financial services, and the ever fickle retail sector.

A dignified mark for one of the leading UK law practices.

In 1985 the legal profession was permitted, albeit in a limited sense, to embark on the unknown and perilous path of 'marketing'. As it is not feasible to market an individual commodity which in perceptual terms does not, except in a generic sense exist, the first logical step must be to establish an identity and in order to effect such a notion, a management decision must be taken. The legal profession collectively faced a serious dilemma; first there was rarely any management structure in place geared to make such a decision (law firms being partnerships rather than companies) and secondly they were individually hesitant of making the first move for fear of opening the floodgates to massive competitive and unnecessary expenditure. Under the fear of competitive pressure, some preliminary decisions were however made, although with scant foreknowledge of the possible consequences.

Design consultancies were duly consulted and unpalatable advice was at the outset usually undigested. The notion of appointing a small caucus committee to steer and approve the consultancy's recommendations (as opposed to all 47 partners being permitted to adjudicate on the house colour) was anathema and contrary to normal procedure; the idea of a collective identity was in any case a dubious proposition, as litigation, property law, company law and divorce were traditionally treated as separate and specialised areas and the tiresome notion of 'cross-selling' was a less than appealing intrusion on an

Professions are perceived as bastions - unassailable and fearsome. Trepidation sets in when circumstances dictate a visit to a doctor, an accountant or a lawyer. Initial responses to external signals are crucial; do I trust these people?; is there a possibility of empathy with the individual to whom I have been assigned?; am I to be stitched up?

An element of humanity, playing on the received culture of our collective preconceived ideas, can open many doors. Dot the 'i's, cross the 't's is what most of us require for our personal security.

Slee
Blackwell
Solicitors

Bird & Bird, a name which evokes an almost irresistible temptation to parody. Resist one must, for this is a respectable, highly revered law practice mainly dealing with the inscrutable area of hi-tech intellectual property. A tiny bird-like substitution for the serif on the ampersand is sufficient to inject some humanity into what otherwise might appear to be a less than human organisation. The device is however used in multiple form to create a textural decoration.

Bastions of the law are being increasingly breached by de-regulation. Accountants and even estate agents are now allowed to trespass on what was once sacred ground. Unwelcome competition perhaps, but a catalyst to image rejuvenation. Ross & Craig, hitherto known as Leonard Ross and Craig, is an ambitious law firm set on an expansion course. There being no particular advantage in being perceived as Jewish, their metamorphosis into a Scottish sounding law firm was achieved by dropping the first part of their name.

Hylton Potts, a tiny law practice for whom small, if not beautiful, is at least design conscious.

Turner Kenneth Brown, a largish practice who were one of the first to grasp the nettle after de-regulation and turn their attention to marketing their expertise. Respectable, established, reliable - all the attributes one would expect from such an organisation have been retained in their visual identity. Designerisms would have not only been anathema to the partners but inappropriate to their market.

ordered and time honoured *modus operandi*.

Through discussions, arguments, frustrations and a painful learning curve there emerged the realisation that within any competitive environment a unique culture, a focused and individual offer, needs not only to be created, consolidated and agreed, but to be communicated. The culture shock of deregulation in the legal profession, forcing as it has the necessity to define individual identities, has provided the platform on which management not only re-defined itself in terms of a more competitive environment, but enabled itself to formulate constructive attitudes with which to achieve its new-found goals. Individual and competitive identities are now becoming a reality in the legal profession, due to management decisions hitherto hardly contemplated being taken under enforced market pressure.

The Move to Visual Relevance
Professional bodies face particular problems in identity terms. Many have been established for a considerable time and are generally less than convinced of the necessity for change. However, the environment in which lawyers, doctors and accountants operate does change and in order to remain relevant, the professional body has to constantly adopt new stances.

Coats of arms abound in these areas as badges of established respectability, but they belong to a visual vernacular which is no longer understood. One coat

54

T K B

LEGAL SERVICES
for the
PUBLIC SECTOR

ROSS
&
CRAIG

BIRD & BIRD

BIRD & BIRD

HYLTON-POTTS

Solicitors

55

Linklaters & Paines, one of the largest UK law firms, developed their identity from the mid-1980s in a somewhat haphazard fashion. Furthermore, with the introduction of a new and sophisticated in-house technology, it was found that the original visual components had insufficient structural strength to be satisfactorily digitised on desktop publishing systems. A new visual identity was therefore developed which was not only designed specifically for the new technology but also moved the visual vernacular of the practice into a more contemporary mode without overtly stating radical change.

of arms looks very much like another to the uninitiated and therefore has little value in terms of differentiation or establishing any unique personality of the organisation it represents. They do however generate considerable internal loyalty, and it is a brave move on the part of management to contemplate their demise.

The Institute of Chartered Management Accountants (ICMA) was founded in 1919 in order to fully comprehend and cope with the growing complexities of the business world - its *raison d'être* remains much the same today. On changing its name to the Chartered Institute of Management Accountants (CIMA) in 1985, the institute took the opportunity to re-examine how it should be perceived by a new generation of business people and translate this into contemporary and relevant visual terms.

As in any other field of endeavour, the institute operates in a highly competitive environment, although as with many professional bodies there was, prior to the outset of the corporate identity exercise, a certain reluctance to acknowledge the fact. Relatively long-established bodies represented by traditional trappings such as coats of arms and mahogany strewn reception areas do tend to exhibit a certain complacency; a fresh approach to the visible face of an organisation can act as a catalyst to re-examining the realities of its position in the market-place and to change its culture accordingly.

The brief, developed jointly by the design consultants and the institute itself was to express function, to emphasise a unique position in the marketplace and to appear relevant, responsive and aware. The elements of the scheme were required to evoke a forward looking organisation based on established tradition but with a strong emphasis on the management aspect which makes CIMA unique among the six chartered bodies of accountants. In simple terms, the specific visual components of the new identity consisted of 'numeratising' the full name of the institute by means of a series of vertical columns, the individual letters being arranged in an arithmetical format; the initial letters of the new name - CIMA - summarised

The
Institute of
Cost and
Management
Accountants

Incorporated by Royal Charter

annual report 1985

ICMA - the Institute of Cost and Management Accountants - complete with coat of arms. Traditional heraldic statements rarely lend an individuality or character to their owners. On the other hand, there is a certain sense of immutable stability inherent in these devices - a factor which presumably keeps the college of heralds in business.

the equation, the *'M'* being italicised in order to emphasise the strong management bias of the organisation.

The two typefaces chosen for general printed matter counterpoint each other, echoing the two faces employed for the central graphic device. The simple upright type in capital letters employed for the full name was leavened by the italic lower case style employed for the management *'M'*. Standard colours, again counterpointed, consisted of a sober navy accented by a sharp but warm red.

Flexibility

The basic CIMA visual statements mean little in themselves; it is the way in which they are assembled, controlled and managed which ensures their effectiveness. Furthermore the institute, having a broad spectrum of target audiences ranging from students to members, from government to big business, needs to be able to focus accurately on these markets. Different visual 'tones of voice' need to be employed, involving considerable manipulation of the basic elements.

Organisations evolve (at least, in order to remain relevant they should); their visual image has therefore to keep pace, to be flexible and capable of development. This requires an on-going commitment on the part of management to the importance of corporate identity and in the case of CIMA this has

CIMA - the Chartered Institute of Management Accountants - a new name, a new visual identity. The ordered system of basic numeracy translated into typography replaces medieval imagery. Management accountancy (as opposed to auditing or finance) is their *raison d'être*, and this is signalled by the traditional typographic ploy of emphasis - italicising.
No symbols or extraneous graphic devices have been employed to garnish the basic scheme.

A coherent identity is not necessarily achieved by applying corporate elements on to everything that moves. Rather, it is the imposition of a stylistic approach to each item which represents the organisation concerned - typographic attitudes, illustration techniques and the use of a controlled colour palette all contribute to the overall projection of an ethos if carefully orchestrated.

Different tones of voice for different target audiences. No identity scheme should be inflexible. Students are as important to CIMA as its eminent Fellows, and need to be addressed in a vernacular sympathetic to their culture.

proved to have been a positive and constructive attitude. The identity has evolved; new visual vernaculars have been created in order to target identified 'niche' markets (students, for example, respond to somewhat different visual stimuli than government ministers) and, given the fact that society itself evolves in terms of its response to visual style, the visual language of the institute needs to correspond to changes in our overall cultural attitudes.

DEVELOPMENT CONTROL

Many far more commercially oriented organisations have failed to grasp this fundamental principle of cultural projection, ossifying their supposedly new-found image in the pages of a rigid design 'bible'. Certain elements of a visual identity should be sacrosanct in order to maintain continuity and stability, but an insidious suspicion of 'yesterday's people' can prevail if continuous reassessment is not exercised.

The mechanisms for the development and control of CIMA's corporate identity were established at the outset, and consist of two basic principles; the appointment of an in-house 'identity guardian' of sufficient seniority to be entirely credible to the organisation as a whole with on-going lines of communication with the design consultancy, and the establishment of a Design Review Body, meeting at regular intervals, consisting of senior management, principal design users and representatives of the design consultancy.

The design guardian ensures that budgets are adhered to and liaison with the design consultancy is maintained. The Design Review Body assesses the progress of the identity programme and ensures that departmental requirements are fulfilled within the context of the overall corporate identity programme.

As an extension of the identity programme, the Portland Place reception area was re-designed, finally dispelling the somewhat fusty image which persisted in the perception of visitors to the Institute.

Two-dimensional graphic material is but a part of projecting an identity. Any organisation consists of its product, the people who create, manufacture and market it and the environment in which it operates. The interaction and stimulus afforded by these elements should, and in the case of CIMA do, add up to something more vibrant and relevant than before the identity programme was instigated. In 1988, the membership increased by 1,000 over the previous highest total and a student growth rate of 10 per cent was recorded. There is increasing evidence that CIMA is now more widely known and recognised as a major influence in management both in the UK and abroad. A flexible yet stable platform has been created on which to build for future growth and influence, but in order to sustain the momentum, continuing

The CIMA reception area. A letter-head may be the first inkling that the uninitiated receive of its sender's persona. The reception area may well be the second, and neither should contradict the other. This is not to imply that corporate symbols should be woven into carpets and printed on to wallpaper. Aesthetic synergy can be achieved more subtly and with a lighter corporate hand than is often evidenced by some large commercial organisations.

commitment to the identity programme remains
essential.

HAMPTONS

'Hamptons'; being the highest
profile company in the residential
sector among the clutch of estate
agents acquired by a powerful
holding company, was selected
as the corporate umbrella image
for the group.

POLITICS

In 1988, British and Commonwealth Holdings decided
to embark on an acquisition path calculated to create
a national chain of estate agencies in both the
commercial and residential sectors. Having already
established a well integrated network of financial
services ranging from mortgage broking to banking
and property interests, this was considered a logical
and synergistic step towards creating a competitive
and interlocking range of services in the property
market. Apart from the more obvious requirement of
creating a forceful presence for the commercial and
residential operations in their respective markets,
certain other specific problems emerged, possibly
unique to this project in their combination, but
individually by no means unusual.

In order to capitalise on the exposure endemic in the
property sector (site boards, media advertising, etc)
both wings of the operation would obviously benefit
in terms of market awareness from being perceived as
connected. However, the very different markets to be
addressed dictated that they should also be perceived
as separate and individual offers - on the surface, a
paradoxical requirement.

The portfolio of acquired companies in both sectors

had, to a greater or lesser degree, built up a customer loyalty base which it would have been imprudent in the short term to risk alienating by a total identity change - an additional complication being that the various companies traditionally addressed a wide variety of market positions.

In management terms the senior members of the companies, most of whom were financial beneficiaries of the acquisitions, were to remain in executive positions in the new structure. Furthermore, as is frequently the case in estate agency, their former companies traded under their individual names - a factor which, human nature being what it is, did not easily facilitate an enforced demise of their personal profiles.

The combination of factors inherent in this project demanded a specific approach; constructive compromise engineered with political sensitivity. The imposition of a blanket identity, however relevant it may have been to the marketplace, would under the circumstances have risked undermining internal morale at the moment when it was most needed. Without total commitment on the part of senior management, no major identity programme can succeed.

Given the constraints, a variety of avenues were open for consideration in order to achieve balanced national dual identities for the residential and commercial

How to stick a clutch of commercial estate agencies together. Do not trample on sensibilities (keep the names, at least for a while). Do not alienate existing customers (ditto). Create a coherent marketing platform from which all will benefit. Three development stages were devised for introduction over a period of time.

sectors: the creation of a new name or names connected and at the same time differentiated by graphic treatment; the retention of existing trading names but endorsed by an umbrella identity; the use of the most appropriate existing company's identity in each sector for all companies.

In the event, a pragmatic but nevertheless effective route which encompassed the profile, political and differentiation requirements was constructed by the judicious use of an existing name. Of all the acquired companies, the one which had achieved the highest pre-acquisition profile and most closely approximated the intended market position of the group was Hampton & Sons. In nomenclature terms, this was therefore chosen as the pivot around which the group identities were constructed.

64

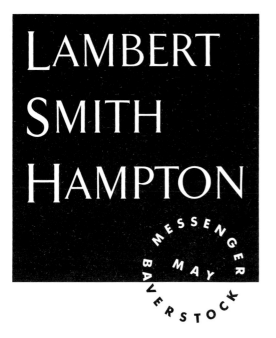

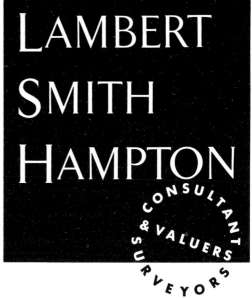

The programme was conceived in two stages; in the residential sector, the existing Hampton & Sons chain became Hamptons, while in the short term the other companies retained their names in a subsidiary role, albeit on occasions in a truncated form; hence Messenger May Baverstock became Hampton Messenger May. A communality of visual treatment ensured an integrated identity. In the medium term, after a period of approximately eighteen months, the subsidiary names would be dropped, leaving a single and by this time focused proposition.

In the commercial sector, Lambert Smith Hampton was selected as the pivotal identity, employing as it does the connecting name in conjunction with the names of the principal protagonists, already established by reputation.

Those companies within the commercial sector group whose reputations were considered crucial to their trading position were visually and in nomenclature terms endorsed by Lambert Smith Hampton, while retaining, in the short term, their existing names.

REPOSITIONING

With any new organisation, management decisions on an identity stance, albeit based on consultancy recommendations, can have profound repercussions in terms of its own culture, how the company develops, and how it is perceived by its markets. The repositioning of an organisation can be a perilous undertaking if the right management decisions are not thoroughly considered in terms of the short- medium- and long-term implications. Extreme clarity is necessary when deciding why such a step should be taken in the first place. The signalling of the appointment of a new chief executive is insufficient reason on its own to commit a company to the expensive cultural upheaval which will ensue.

There are a raft of reasons why a company should consider a repositioning exercise; its image may have become irrelevant through inattention to evolving its identity in tune with its markets; the nature of the company itself may have changed, but not adequately communicated; in the case of a company intending a floatation, it may be that its customers are correctly targeted, but no attention has been paid to projecting an appropriate ethos to the City; or simply that the customer base has shifted either in its composition or in its demands.

F International, a computer programming company established at the beginning of the software boom 25 years ago, based its operating structure on a constructive and relatively revolutionary premise; that the massive wastage of professional women's involvement in business and industry caused by their family obligations could be reversed and indeed tapped. The key to realising this notion was the fact that computer technology had developed to the point where networking had become a feasible proposition, thereby facilitating the positive interaction of staff in locations as disparate as Glasgow and Guildford. Furthermore, the hardware necessary to construct the programs could easily be installed on a kitchen table. The company became highly successful, employing over a thousand married women working from their own homes, providing software packages to government departments, local authorities, financial institutions and retail distribution companies.

In order to develop and expand the company, a decision was taken to plan for a floatation; to this end a research programme was instigated to determine how the company was perceived by its customers, by the City and by its employees, to establish the strengths and weaknesses of operation and investigate how adjustments could be made to sharpen its performance. The findings were salutary.

The name itself was considered obscure and misleading, especially in the light of the fact that the company had by this time closed down its operations outside the UK. 'F' was thought by some to represent 'female' while by others 'freelance' (the latter being in fact the founder's intention). In any event, neither application was thought to be particularly positive. A preponderance of female staff had no special merit and was thought by some sections of the City to be somewhat cranky and the freelance nature of the operation did not inspire confidence that projects would be tightly controlled. The business was, however, perceived to be both efficient and innovative by those who had experienced its services.

In the light of some of the misgivings which surfaced from the research, various management decisions were triggered, among which was to examine ways in which the company could be presented in a more cogent and less ambiguous manner. In order to minimise the danger of alienating existing customers or damaging a profile which had been established since the company's inception, it was decided to maintain elements of the name while at the same time diminishing the obscurity which surrounded it. 'F International' therefore became 'FI Group PLC' with an explanatory strap line which re-explained the initial letters and re-defined the company; 'Flexible Information Systems'.

In visual terms, it was decided to further echo the company's function and ethos by expressing both the networking and the logic endemic in the construction of software programs. This was achieved by superimposing grid lines on every item emanating from the company. These lines visually explained the proportion and geometric structure of, say, a sheet of letter paper or a calling card. An annual report would visibly retain the guide lines used for designing the typography, while signage exposed its structural characteristics.

Secondary visual considerations were the substitution of computer cursors for the full points between the company's initials and the overall colour palette, calculated to be sexually neutral, was confined to the dark blue/purple spectrum.

The specific management requirement to re-launch and re-define an organisation which had in some respects lost its way, was achieved with no loss of existing goodwill or recognition.

F·I·GROUP PLC

Signage echoing a basic corporate statement.

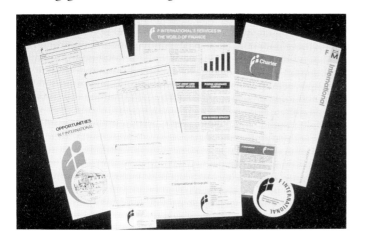

FI International before re-naming or re-design.

69

The FI Software Group is about structured networking, the geometry of programming. It is also about explanations, finding solutions to logistical problems and controlling their application. Leonardo was obsessed with structural explanation - as is Richard Rogers with his inside-out building concepts, exteriorising structure.

Mondrian, too, turns structure into a virtue, but using tone and colour to support his vision, while Gutenberg's bible is still one of the finest examples of perfectly structured and proportioned typography. The notion of creating a visual identity programme reliant largely on the exteriorisation of structure stemmed from these ideas.

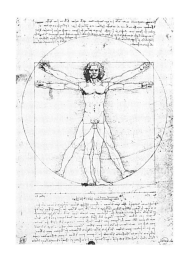
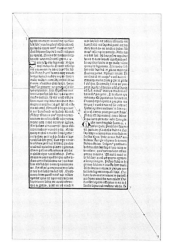

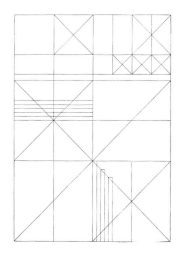
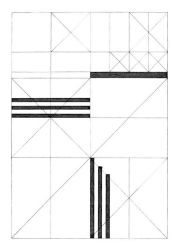

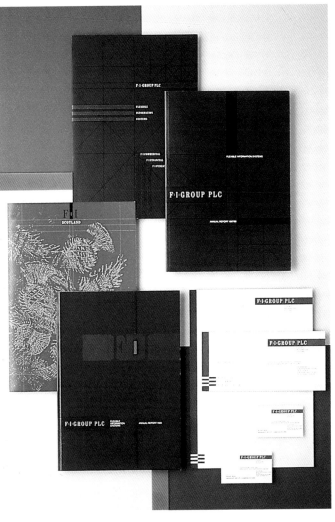

Every scrap of paper can be structurally explained. A4 size, for example, has a peculiarity which, if divided into square sections, leaves disturbing gaps which can be exploited, Mondrian-like, by in-filling with colour.

Typography grids are related to the page for which they are designed - if left on the printed page they offer a structural explanation of their environment.

Because there are an infinite number of ways in which the same object can be explained, an infinite variety of design solutions can be applied to the same scrap of paper - a flexible but nevertheless coherent visual identity system, not reliant on overt symbology.

Endorsement can be heavy - handed or considerate, insistent or excessive, depending upon the purpose which it is supposed to serve. Endorsement for its own sake or the promotion of a holding company's ego is rarely useful, cluttering perceptions of the main message. In the case of the Arts Council, however, the *raison d'être* of the visual identity programme revolved around endorsement - a method whereby organisations as disparate as the Royal Opera or the Scunthorpe Players could be perceived as being part of the Council's largesse without visual interference with their own publicity material.

72

VULNERABILITY

A decision to reposition perceptions of an organisation can be influenced by the need to be defensive, offensive, or in some circumstances both, in the sense that attack can be the best form of defence. Vulnerability to unwelcome takeovers has over recent years become an everyday boardroom hazard and one which is increasingly being addressed by the instigation of a corporate identity programme as an aid to shifting or focusing the way in which a company is regarded. Long established companies which have grown into new market-places either organically or by acquisition are often still perceived as their founders intended - hence, although De La Rue is a world leader in currency management and printing, it is still best known to certain sections of the community as manufacturers of playing cards (which it has not in fact produced for 30 years). This kind of misconception, if not corrected, contributes to a blurred and unstable image suggesting takeover and asset stripping possibilities from outside.

In 1988/9 British and Commonwealth Holdings suffered a significant drop in its share price due to a down-turn in the property market - this was largely due to the fact that its Hampton chain of estate agents projected the highest profile of all their interests, even though representing less than 2 per cent of its portfolio - resulting in a serious misconception by the City of British and Commonwealth's actual worth.

A flexible solution to the Theatre Museum's visual identity based on a full, three and single motif. The figures, representing aspects of the performing arts, were produced by feeding a variety of original material - photographs, banners, poster engravings, drawings, etc into a computer and reducing each image to a monochromatic pixellated form in order to achieve a uniform treatment. Colour was added 'on screen' and a print-out used for artwork. In addition, monochrome and three-colour versions were produced for circumstances where full colour was either inappropriate or too expensive to reproduce. The stage motif can be used for a variety of applications.

Since that time, B&C has collapsed due primarily to the failure of Atlantic Computers, one of its largest subsidiaries. However, the knock-on effect of this was to some degree aggravated by a confused identity policy. Most of B&C's subsidiaries traded under non-B&C names, but some, such as British and Commonwealth Merchant Bank (BCMB), did not. Banks depend on confidence for their existence and although BCMB was trading successfully prior to the collapse of Atlantic, the welter of publicity in the financial press given to B&C's misfortunes ensured that the bank was also sucked into the vortex.

In the case of large and complex holding companies, it could be argued that it is in any event unwise to centralise nomenclature for trading subsidiaries. In the volatile world of financial services, any break-up of the overall group, even if for positive reasons, is complicated by components trading under the original holding company name.

Solutions to problems of this nature are inevitably complex, require the accurate projection of the operating companies to their respective markets while ensuring that the holding company is correctly represented to the comparatively narrow world of the City.

A further aspect of defence against vulnerability is that due to the birthrate down-turn in the 1960s and 1970s there is, recessions notwithstanding, a potential deficiency in suitable graduate recruits into industries and professions of every denomination. Competition among employers is always intense, but it is estimated that within the next five years, demand for professional staff will rise by 17.5 per cent, scientists and engineers by 21 per cent, managers by 12 per cent.

The considered definition of corporate identity will, given the similarity of product or service within many sectors, become a crucial factor in deciding which company to join. It will be the perceived culture, the ethos, the personality of organisations which will give the edge and management will be obliged to take decisions on the question of identity in the relatively short term if in the medium and long term they are not to find themselves bereft of staff.

TONES OF VOICE

The 1980's proliferation of large-scale takeovers and mergers exposed managers to extremely complicated decisions in terms of identity from both commercial and political standpoints. A holding company set on an expansion or acquisition path will be concerned with financial, market and cultural synergies to a greater or lesser degree, dictated by pragmatic considerations.

A centrally controlled group of companies may need to present on the one hand a coherent and integrated image to the financial institutions in the City, while on the other its operating companies may by necessity require individual and niche targeted profiles in the marketplace. The management decisions in these situations are fraught with political and perceptual nuances, not only in operational terms, but in how these relationships should be presented to maximum advantage.

One face to the City, another to the consumer; multi-faceted tones of voice, speaking in a variety of visual languages targeted to a broad spectrum of recipients, each with his own expectations.

The housewife has no interest in the identity of the manufacturer of her favourite washing powder, only the brand; the City, on the other hand, will gauge the financial potential of Unilever on its perspicacity in producing relevant and successful products for its marketplace, however diverse they may appear to the consumer. The endorsement factor in identity terms needs to be handled with extreme care.

Perception analysis of a complicated network of market penetrations on a variety of levels, leading to the conclusion that WH Smith needed a holding company identity which was different from its core business for the exclusive consumption of the financial institutions. The City needs to know that WH Smith owns Our Price Records (a largely teenage market) and for that matter Waterstones (specialist book shops); it is preferable, on the other hand, that the consumer does not (WH Smith being middle of the road). WH Smith is one of the most successful retail chains in the UK, filling as it has a wide variety of market sectors on the high street ranging from up-

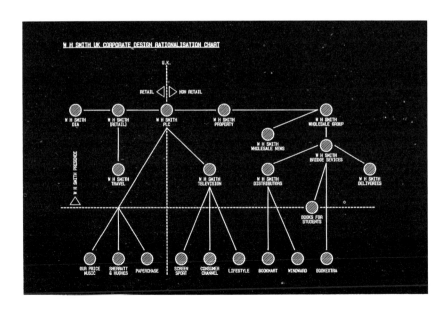

In the volatile financial climate of the mid-1980s WH Smith became somewhat vulnerable to takeover, in part due to an ignorance in the City of the exact nature of the company. Its core High Street retailing business, having the highest profile, tended to represent the company as a whole in terms of activity and ethos. In reality its interests were far-ranging, encompassing cable television, general wholesale, publishing, DIY, travel, property and specialist record and book chains in the UK, Europe and North America.

With a long tradition of market awareness and the use of corporate identity as a marketing and positioning tool, the company decided to take corrective action by commissioning a study, first to establish ways in which the holding company should be correctly represented to the City and secondly to create an endorsement policy for its operating companies. The central notion of this exercise was the construction of a Matrix, delineating on the one hand the degree of 'Smithness' relevant to each operating company's market and on the other the nature of each business in terms of retail, non-retail and City perceptions. It was, for example, decided that in spite of certain profile advantages which could be gained for the holding company by endorsement of all its operations, the downside easily outweighed this proposition in a number of instances. A chain of specialist record shops aimed at the teenage market would suffer a considerable loss of credibility with its

market specialist book shops to teenage record stores. The central core business however remains middle of the road catch-all. Consumer perception has necessarily to be segmented; while it may be acceptable for WH Smith customers to buy their weekend DIY facilities at 'Do It All', it is problematic that the latest popular music idol's new release will be sought at WH Smith - or indeed if acquired at that outlet, its containing plastic bag will signal a contradictory culture of the consumer. The City, on the other hand, needs to know the extent of WH Smith's market penetration; a conundrum solved by the careful and considered use of endorsement.

A new logotype for the WH Smith's holding company - only ever seen by the City - removing its perception of WH Smith as a single operation company.

customers if perceived to be part of the core retail business whose market had little relevance to the offer; likewise, a chain of up-market specialist book shops would not retain its niche if seen to be connected to its middle-market parent.

However, the City is also a customer, and ignorance of Smith's carefully structured penetration of the overall market did not assist in its comprehension of its strengths. A situation which had unwittingly emerged during the company's period of expansion was that the identity of the holding company was the same as that of the core retail business, thereby narrowing perception of its activities. It was therefore decided that a new identity should be created for the holding company specifically for use on communication material directed at the City such as annual reports and financial press releases. This, while retaining some recall to its predecessor, would signal its pre-eminence and dispel suspicions of its reliance on a single offer. The management decision to instigate this exercise was largely based on its experience of the potential inherent in well considered identity programmes, both as a catalyst and an implementation tool for major corporate decisions.

MARKETING DUALITY

It is not infrequent that the different activities of an organisation are in some form of conflict.
The WH Smith example of separating perceptions of

the operating and holding companies was a logical market-led decision, and was taken as corrective action. In the case of an entirely new company, the opportunity exists from the outset to avoid any sensitive conflicts which may occur during the organisation's future development. In 1988, a company named Gaia was formed to exploit a highly complex but efficient currency exposure and investment management system which had been developed over some years by an individual consultant operating from Canada and Holland. The ultimate *raison d'être* however, was to plough back profits from the operation into an independently funded sister organisation concerned with world ecological improvement.

There were therefore two distinct operations, though obviously linked in purpose; to the outside world and for that matter to the respective markets, neither activity had anything whatsoever to do with the other except to a few influential bodies which would eventually be involved in the development of the end purpose.

The name Gaia, the mythical earth goddess, was chosen as the central name for both companies, Gaiacorp being the financial management wing, the Gaia Trust being concerned with financing and controlling the ecological development activities. For Gaiacorp a high degree of stability and credibility needed to be established in a field which few

Gaia, the earth goddess, might on the surface be considered an unlikely bedfellow for Lucre. However, banknotes are the stuff of currency management (the activity of Gaiacorp) and the goddess is a fitting figurehead for the Gaia Trust (the distributor of Gaiacorp's profits in the cause of ecological reconstruction). Gaia drawn in the manner of banknote portraiture does after all seem apposite, though interestingly paradoxical.

institutions fully understand, although in fact for many companies currency exposure management is probably one of the most important sources of profit improvement. The company needed to communicate to the City, the institutions and the investment and pension fund managers. For the City a depiction of the goddess was employed as a background visual device - but rendered as she might be on a currency note. Typographic treatment is restrained, elegant yet contemporary. Visual punctuation is achieved by the use of bank note details. Overall, a positive aura of financial expertise. For the Gaia Trust, the goddess is brought to the fore, as the symbol of ecological responsibility.

The philosophy behind this separation was simply that the City, the principal market for Gaiacorp, might view with some suspicion an organisation apparently dedicated to the environment. The activities of the two operations have different management structures, different offices and different individual goals; a requirement for related but differentiated images. In the long term, the connection will need to be established in order to lend financial credibility to the Trust. In identity terms, two seemingly incompatible activities are being handled in a sensitive but direct manner - avoiding possible negatives while creating a coherent totality.

Three thousand forms in thirty different formats is a logistical nightmare which should not happen to anybody. It does, however. Large companies tend to spawn small empires and if not centrally controlled they will manufacture their own communication systems independently of any thought for overall continuity.

The chance to unravel such a situation and eliminate such anomalies as duplication and format incompatibility is presented by the instigation of a visual identity programme. In this instance, the number of forms was reduced by half, and sizes rationalised to the simple 'A' system while considerable savings were achieved in print costs.

RATIONALISATION

Although systems rationalisation is rarely the primary motivation for management to take the visual identity reorganisation path, one tangible logistical benefit which can be identified from such a step is that of communications improvement. An important part of any corporate identity programme will be an audit of all visual material - among which will be internal communications systems. Over a period of time, it is not unusual for a plethora of duplication of forms, memos and directives to occur - all regarded as essential to the organisation of individual departments, but with little regard for the overall communications network. While re-designing these items into a corporate style, it is not only their function which can be rationalised into a more efficient and coherent format, but duplication can be eliminated.

During the original corporate identity exercise for WH Smith, some three thousand forms in over thirty formats in use by the company were rationalised to less than eighteen hundred in only two formats. The print savings effected by a design rationalisation of this nature can amortise the fees involved within a year. A spin-off management advantage not to be ignored.

MANAGEMENT BUY-OUT

Management buy-outs can be complicated in terms of identity and positioning. The extent of value inherent in the 'parent's' reputation and profile needs to be

82

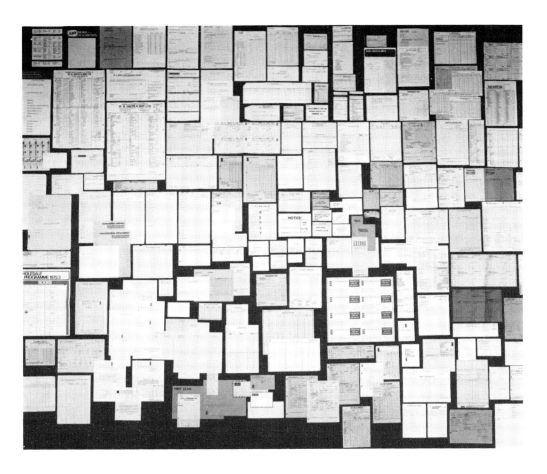

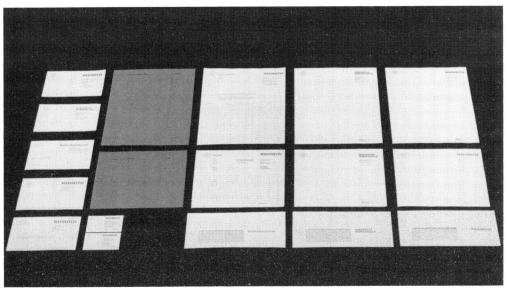

83

carefully assessed when considering ways in which to launch and project the new company. This can range from a desire to incorporate certain legally allowable aspects of the original organisation's image to a deliberate decision to eschew all connections and present an entirely new identity. By definition, it is likely that at least some elements of the original company's make-up will not be compatible with the ethos and image of the new structure and these will need to be identified.

Hornes Corporate Clothing, a division of Sears PLC, was subject to a buy-out in order to combine manufacturing and marketing into a single entity. Its products are at the quality end of the corporate clothing sector but additionally, due to the contribution of the manufacturing side which was not previously part of Hornes, in the 'own label' market. The *raison d'être* of the new company was therefore more broadly based than the original, which effectively negated any advantage to be gleaned by signalling its origins in any overt form.

From both the legal and marketing standpoints, a new name needed to be established. In order to capitalise on an existing reputation in the own label market, Wensum, the name of an obscure river which runs near the main factory in Norfolk and already in use representing the manufacturing operation, was chosen to represent the company as a whole. In marketing terms, Wensum is by no means

BY APPOINTMENT TO
H. M. QUEEN ELIZABETH II
LIVERY TAILORS
THE WENSUM COMPANY PLC
LONDON

Coats of arms, so far somewhat denigrated by this writer, do have their place in the contemporary scheme of things. They do not, however, often sit happily with other visual identity components. In this instance, the identity was designed after the granting of the warrant, thereby dictating a degree of visual synergy between the two elements.

an ideal name, it being obscure, visually unattractive and less than sonorous. The decision, however, was made on the grounds of 'a bird in the hand' and an inability to agree on an alternative.

This presented certain constraints on the creation of the visual identity. In addition, a Royal Warrant had been inherited from the original company and needed to be incorporated into any visual scheme.

An intertwined 'W' motif was devised as the main visual element, thereby negating the necessity to visually emphasise the shortcomings of the name while at the same time creating a device sympathetic to the heraldic coat of arms of the Warrant. Colour differentiation was employed to delineate the divisions - holding, manufacturing and marketing - while the careful use of typography ensures that the overtly traditional approach is tempered by contemporariness.

The visual solution was dictated by a series of management decisions based, for better or worse, on pragmatism; it was decided that no overt connection with the original company had to be perceived and that the Royal Warrant was to be a major marketing tool. These requirements in themselves should not present any serious problems to the design consultant. In the event, the chosen name was, in my opinion, inappropriate. The reasons, however, were, in human terms, comprehensible (a decision on the part of the directors to neutralise any suspicion of hierarchial management by the use of their own names in any specific order).

The brief, even if open to question, is paramount, even if not perfect in marketing terms; it is the prerequisite responsibility of the consultant to understand the nature of the client and his markets. It is also often the case that sympathy for client attitudes, even if not exactly parallel with those propounded by the consultant, by necessity needs to be a factor in arriving at an optimum solution.

Research and analysis can point to certain directions and form the bedrock on which management decisions can be made. In the final analysis however, it must be assumed that the client knows how to run his own business. In this case, the visual identity does succeed in expressing the ethos and purpose of the company, but more in spite, rather than because, of an original decision.

PUBLIC RELATIONS

Halfords, a retail chain which in the early 1970s was
perceived as being little more than a corner cycle
shop, decided to shift their market penetration into
auto spares, it having recently been acquired by an
international oil company. Branch managers however,
on whom the lifeblood of the business depended,
remained unconvinced that this strategy was viable,
Halfords having been a long-established family
business concerned with the more leisurely trade of
bicycles and their accessories. Nevertheless, a new
visual identity was devised in order to reflect the new
owners' synergistic ambitions and, prior to any public
exposure, a mass gathering of some four hundred
branch managers was arranged in a Birmingham
theatre where they were to be exposed to the new
strategy in detail, supported by illustrations as to how
this would be reflected to their customers.

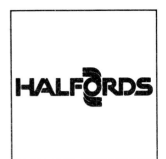

As the chief executive happened to be a member of
the Magic Circle, the proceedings opened with his
own conjuring act, performed in the manner of a
warm-up prior to a TV quiz show. This was followed
by a 'TV personality' outlining the future directions
for the company. The *pièce de resistance* however was a
programmed ten projector split screen presentation of
the new visual identity. A standing ovation ensued,
ensuring the future loyalty and dedication to a
concept previously viewed with some suspicion. This
in normal circumstances may appear to be a trifle
excessive in the interests of internal public relations,

Light music out of heavy weather. Although the notion that composers should be recompensed for the use of their work on television or radio is perfectly acceptable, restaurants and hairdressers are understandably less enthusiastic about having to pay a levy for the right to lull their customers with a radio or hi-fi. A sympathetic and up-beat image is therefore called for, if for no other reason than to inject some joy into the transaction. PRS's previous visual identity was, to say the least, forbidding and furthermore misleading, both in nomenclature and visual terms (a television screen representing an audio discipline?).

One of the longest established department stores in the UK, but by the late 1980s sadly in decline due to the previous owners' neglect and the onslaught of niche market retail offers of the period.
In order to survive, new attitudes new management, new marketing techniques were essential and these needed to be strongly signalled. One of the differentiating characteristics of a department store is that it is usually vertical rather than horizontal. Images of escalators and lifts - shoppers moving up and down rather than sideways. The name lends itself to a vertical treatment in this instance and satisfactory conveys the nature of the offer. Colour plays a crucial role in this scheme, suggesting as it does a move up-market while making a contemporary statement.

The Commonwealth Development Corporation masquerading as a government department akin to the Inland Revenue and the representation of its change of attitude to being major competitors to the World Bank.

GIVING MUSIC ITS DUE

OWEN OWEN

DEPARTMENT STORE

When Burmah Oil acquired the ailing Halfords corner shop bicycle retail chain, its intention was to transform the offer into auto-spares, in direct competition to Unipart and the like. Halfords was a traditional family business, with all that that implies. Initially, Burmah imposed an embargo on selling no other motor oil than Castrol, one of its leading products. With the culture shock of new ownership and direction coupled with perceived restructure edicts from on high, the branch managers - some four hundred of them at the time - were perhaps understandably in a state of pique and low morale.

The psychological pivot around which the crucial acceptance by the managers of Burmah's strategy was the introduction of an own brand product to set alongside the Castrol brand.

This the patrons accepted as being expedient both politically and from a marketing standpoint. A new corporate identity was a reality and needed to be visually expressed to the consumer and employees alike. But it was the oil can which sold it.

90

but in the event the result more than justified the means.

The public launch of a new visual identity provides a raft of public relations and profile opportunities. Witness the weekly quality business press coverage; four column photographs of chief executives posing in front of their shiny new logos more often than not wrought in stainless steel.

The annual general meeting provides a pad from which to launch new directions (providing the figures are not overly gloomy) or, for certain organisations such as trade unions, the annual conference is the ideal platform, given the media coverage which accompanies such events. The expense involved in creating a special launch will obviously be greater than if an already scheduled gathering is exploited for this purpose. However, if the new identity genuinely signals a new direction, it is likely that the public relations advantages to be gained would justify the mounting of a major event.

IDENTITY ADJUSTMENT

Any identity programme which purports to set the ingredients in stone is in danger of ossifying the development of the company it represents. Companies which rely on targeted consumer trends are particularly vulnerable to finding themselves out of step with developing or shifting markets unless

From cosy Italy to Mediterranean alfresco - a repositioning exercise carried out in order to target a changing market. Eating habits are volatile. There was a day when pizza was firmly locked inside Italy and hamburgers were something only served up in 1940s black and white American movies. Now, these commodities are as much a part (or perhaps more) of the Anglo-Saxon culture as kippers and pickled walnuts.

they take a flexible view of how they present themselves.

Pastificio, owned at the time by Grand Metropolitan, was the first fresh pasta restaurant of its kind to be introduced in the UK. With its original design concept the chain achieved considerable success, but by 1988 its 26 restaurants were facing increased mid-market competition and the company felt that the original Italianate interiors and the family oriented visual identity no longer conveyed the right image to the customer.

The new design solution was to be evolutionary, not revolutionary: building on, rather than radically changing Pastificio's established personality. The restaurants needed to stand out more alongside strongly branded competitors, and to be perceived as a 'Mediterranean' experience with somewhat more sophistication in its graphic re-presentation.

As a result of consumer research, the new concept stresses an alfresco, relaxed mood. The logotype was adjusted rather than redesigned, and complemented with a stylised illustration emphasising a holiday atmosphere. On installation of the evolved concept, the company reported an increase in revenue of 15 per cent and the scheme gained a Design Effectiveness Award from the Design Business Association.

In a volatile market situation, a repositioning exercise

A pizza is, generally speaking, a pizza and it is the style and ambience in which it is to be consumed which will either attract or repel the consumer.

can tempt radicalism. Management in this instance avoided throwing any babies out with the bathwater by their circumspection, and were duly rewarded.

NEW FOR OLD

Long-established companies, though blessed with a certain credibility which comes with age, frequently become unfocused in terms of the changing nature of the markets with which they deal. Furthermore, younger competitors are naturally enough often fresher, more relevant and dynamic in their approach and can quickly erode the more established company's market share if decisions are not taken to counter the onslaught. The acquisition of smaller companies perceived as representing the new guard is often a route taken by long-established firms wishing to increase their relevance. The danger here is that the new blood simply becomes absorbed into the old, creating a yet more moribund organisation. Often, it takes a radical management decision, involving a change of key personnel, in order to effect any meaningful change of direction for a company which has, over many years, lost its way. A new corporate identity will achieve nothing if it does not represent the reality of a new direction.

The companies which form the Toplis and Harding Group are the descendants of a business started in 1790. Since that time, it has grown, through organic expansion and acquisition, to be among the world's

Wisdom, an attribute of some rarity, but one which is essential to adjudication. An enthroned Solomonesque figure sits in judgement within a seal of approval reflecting, perhaps, upon disasters ahead. The Toplis Group are loss adjusters - that is to say that when disaster strikes there is an inevitable gulf between the insurer and the insured as to the amount of recompense due. This has to be refereed by the adjuster.

Pastiche, unlike parody, is a stylistic consideration, recalling other times or other cultures. The deliberately heraldic approach to this device with its invented motto does lend authority to an organisation whose honesty and integrity must be above suspicion.

largest claims-handling organisations, employing over one thousand people in 143 offices throughout the world.

Due to rapid growth and some diversification during the latter part of this century, the organisation had become somewhat unfocused. The consultancy task was to rationalise the divisional names, reflecting the management's restructuring exercise and to create a strong visual communality throughout the group. The traditional long-established nature of the company had to be preserved, but with a new dynamic relevant to its markets.

Loss adjusters generally speaking deal with disasters - a somewhat unusual commodity - but one which, under the circumstances requires a degree of *gravitas*. The pivotal device around which the new world-wide identity is built is a 'seal' depicting a seated figure signifying authority and judgement reinforced by a surrounding motto - 'Integrity & Equity' - deliberately an example of 'new heraldry', but in this case entirely apposite. The presentation of marketing and information literature counterpoints the 'pastiche' approach to the seal by its contemporariness both in typographic and illustrative terms. Some companies within the group retain their original names, their specialist associations being long-established. Others, perhaps the less successful ones, have changed to the parent name. In all cases, their visual style is centralised, endorsed by wisdom, integrity and equity.

A change of pace for any organisation can be a painful experience for many of its members. Old orders are comfortable and reassuring and command a high degree of loyalty. Market forces, however, dictate that shifts in management style, structures, attitudes and goals are necessary in order to remain relevant and to progress. These shifts need to be communicated but with sympathy and regard for heritage.

'Established in 1790' or a Royal Warrant coat of arms, devices often incorporated in companies' images, do communicate longevity and reliability. While there is no reason to abandon such messages, they are generally insufficient on their own or in their original form to signal relevance to today's commercial conditions.

REPUTATIONS

In 1988, the British and Commonwealth Merchant Bank decided to exploit a particular financial phenomenon which had, prior to the stock market crash of 1987, created a serious vacuum for the private investor. City based stockbrokers, during the frantic activity following the 'Big Bang' deregulation of 1986, had channelled their marketing and operational activities exclusively toward the institutional investor, leaving the private stock holder with little support or interest from the major players. A substantial slice of disillusioned disposable capital was beached, and therefore available for more individual attention.

Consequently, a decision was made to establish a nationwide network of small and medium sized provincial stockbrokers, linked to a centralised system of established. City involvement, offshore banking and international investment opportunities.

In order to communicate this enhanced proposition to the acquired brokers' existing private clients and create a credible offer to which either the disaffected or 'new wealth' potential clients would respond, an integrated identity needed to be established.

The holding company, the British and Commonwealth Merchant Bank, was not automatically considered to be an appropriate appellation for what was essentially intended to be a personalised service and it was therefore decided that a research programme be instigated in order to determine the direction to be taken in terms of both naming policy and visual tone. Existing and potential clients, the prime movers in the individual companies and key city personnel were interviewed in order to assess their response to a variety of propositions. These ranged from the notion of adopting the holding company's existing identity (not previously associated with stockbroking) to purloining one of the acquired companies' names, through to the possibility of creating an entirely new offer which could be freshly targeted but without the immediate benefit of established credentials.

Precedents not having been established in this field,

STOCK GROUP

An investment decision on the part of an individual requires a high degree of confidence. Tradition, solidity, caution and wisdom are the attributes most cherished by the private investor. No off-the-wall graphic tricks here. Although a newly formed company assembled through acquisition, the notion that it had been trading for hundreds of years with no discernible hiccups was a prime consideration in the construction of the visual identity. Restrained, responsible, but nevertheless with contemporary overtones, is the message. Veracity is not compromised, the constituent parts of the organisation in themselves being already established in an acceptable vein. To the designer, this visual solution may appear to be something of a non-event, but it is a deliberate understatement.

STOCK GROUP

STOCK BEECH & CO LTD
STOCKBROKERS

Keith Yeates
General Manager

SPECTRUM
BOND STREET BRISTOL BS1 3DE
TELEPHONE: 0272-260051 FACSIMILE: 0272-253278 TELEX: 44739
A MEMBER OF THE INTERNATIONAL STOCK EXCHANGE A MEMBER OF THE SECURITIES ASSOCIATION

there was little on which the design consultant could base recommendations without a thorough assessment of the market and its reaction to the proposed offer. An analysis of the response suggested the route which was eventually adopted: to embrace at least part of the most appropriate and respected name from the clutch of acquired companies as the main proposition (the Stock Group); to visualise this in restrained but nevertheless contemporary terms; to retain existing company names in a subsidiary capacity and to endorse the overall operation with the holding company's reputation as it existed at the time.

A complicated but not impossible brief for a design solution, but one which could not have been arrived at without targeted research, the parameters of which were contrived to facilitate a relevant visual hierarchy which would maximise the value of the various marketing advantages.

Ironically, the success of this particular operation led to serious problems when the parent company failed, it being a valuable asset needing to be realised. In the event, it was sold off, ensuring its survival. However, if an original decision had been made to use the British and Commonwealth name, the situation might have been irretrievable; the obverse of the circumstances of the bank's problems described earlier.

CLARITY OF FUNCTION

It is not infrequent that an organisation becomes so familiar with its own culture and visual expressions that it becomes ingrained to the exclusion of any realisation as to how outsiders may perceive its function. Halfords, for example, used to refer to one of its product groupings as 'ice'. The notion that this referred to 'in-car entertainment' only became apparent after somewhat embarrassed enquiries from new employees.

More serious is a situation when an organisation itself appears in an ambiguous light. The Performing Right Society (PRS) might reasonably be supposed to be concerned with the rights of performers. Not so. Its *raison d'être* is in fact to collect royalties on behalf of composers and lyricists. Furthermore, its visual identity centred around what appeared to be a television screen - normally associated with visual performance rather than audio composition. It has two quite separate target groups - the composers themselves (recruitment) and those from whom their royalties are collected (a degree of coercion).

Although within the music industry the function of PRS is generally understood, there existed some serious problems with the users - a typical riposte might be that they were not going to pay twice (having previously, perhaps, contributed in some form to the performers' remuneration).

Management decided to take the opportunity of its 75th anniversary to re-launch the organisation in a more cogent and sympathetic form. The television screen was therefore abandoned and replaced by a full colour five line stave representative of the joy rather than the pain of transmitting music. This three dimensionally delineated the organisation's initials; the full name, in itself confusing, being relegated to a merely legal status. An explanatory strap line was devised 'giving music its due' which, visually joined to the stave device by the use of a music bracket, contributed to communicating the society's function.

Names, symbols, colours, in fact whole identities often evolve over a period of time without any central realisation of their effect on the outside world. Executives and staff alike are lulled into a comfortable but blinkered perception of themselves which is often at considerable variance with an outsider's attitudes and it takes some courage to accept and act upon an external objective view.

GIVING MUSIC ITS DUE

PRS is now regarded more sympathetically by its target audience and its members; one well-known composer in particular, having hitherto refused to join on the grounds that he previously perceived the society as being a trade union, has since joined now that the organisation's function has been clarified. Internally there is an increased sense of purpose and cohesion and the general public is more aware of the society's existence.

A CAREER IN TAXATION

An Introduction for Graduates

JUNE 1991

THE INSTITUTE
OF TAXATION

A new identity for The Institute of Taxation. A balance between the organisation's desire to be both traditionally responsible and contemporarily relevant.

4   The Critical Path

CHOICE OF CONSULTANCY

When the need for an identity programme has been identified and the management decision taken to proceed, a *modus operandi* needs to be established, the appointment of a suitable consultancy being the first priority. The number of consultancies claiming expertise in corporate identity has burgeoned since the late 1960s and the choice is now bewildering.

Advertising versus Design

Perhaps one of the classic confusions to the uninitiated is the precise function of the design consultancy as opposed to the advertising agency. In the 1950s, before the advent of the 'design consultancy' as it is now known, advertising agencies offered face lift operations as part of their strategic package. As the value of defining and expressing corporate personality became realised, specialist consultancies outside the agency framework were established, and advertising became more focused on the promotion of brands. Recently there has been a trend for large advertising groups to buy back into corporate identity consultancy by acquiring companies whose speciality it is. Generally speaking, these companies are left intact to pursue their specific function, their ownership being more or less irrelevant in so far as the client is concerned.

On the other hand, the spate of takeovers and mergers in the design world during the late 1980s, mostly orchestrated by advertising groups, has gone some way to rationalising the way in which the industry works and has provided the 'one stop shop' notion. However, it must be said that this scenario might be thought by some to reduce the originality and design integrity inherent in the independent consultancy.

The Mix

The consultancy's role in the creation and implementation of a successful corporate identity, although pivotal, is but a part of the whole. In addition to the commitment both in terms of management and financial resources of the company itself, other outside agencies need to be integrated into the process. Public relations consultancies' role in launching the programme is crucial, but their on-going involvement in emphasising and developing the new culture is of equal importance. Advertising agencies, handling as they do the highest profile media exposure of the corporate ethos, obviously need to be completely in tune with the identity programme.

Curiously and perhaps unfortunately this is rarely the case. As stated earlier, historically companies would automatically seek guidance on questions of identity

A project for updating the Advertising Standards Authority's visual image. Although commissioned on a competitive basis, the solution was never implemented due, perhaps, to a final reluctance to disturb the *status quo*.

A reasonably successful result of collaboration between a design consultancy, a public relations company and an advertising agency.

from advertising agencies - they are, after all, concerned with visual exposure and communication. However, although a few agencies have made attempts at creative visual identities for their clients, the results have generally been superficial, based as one would expect on current and perhaps ephemeral marketplace perceptions. With the design profession's growth into this specialised area, advertising agencies' involvement has declined, and a degree of resentment has developed from within the advertising industry with a tendency to marginalise the importance of corporate identity as a major plank in the construction and projection of corporate culture.

It could be argued that agencies' purpose is to promote products and services, to identify and target markets and that concern with the corporate ethos of the producer is irrelevant to that purpose. It could also be argued that the product *is* the company; that the quality, uniqueness and character inherent in the product is interactive with the company from which it stems. If this is the case, the agency needs to understand the design consultancy's direction for the identity of the company and the design consultancy needs to understand the agency's aspirations for the product.

This would suggest that the two protagonists should collaborate at the early stages of corporate identity gestation and continue to do so during its development - an arrangement which is unfortunately rarely realised, often resulting in contradictory visual elements being stitched together in product

106

advertising. The company logo dropped into the bottom of a full page advertisement is not evidence of coherent endorsement.

Although corporate advertising and product advertising should not be confused (the consumer is not buying the company, the employees and the City not necessarily buying the product) there are obvious advantages to be gained from a synergy being established between the two.

In the extreme, an advertising campaign can sell the product by selling the company, as in the case of BP, where an elaborate and successful series of television commercials did not mention petrol; rather, with the backing of a new visual identity, the emphasis was laid on its international influence, its Britishness, its integrity and its responsibility towards the environment. Its market share increased because motorists felt more comfortable with BP, though making what is after all a distress purchase of a product which in no way differs from its competitors.

CRITERIA FOR APPOINTMENT

The criteria on which an appointment should be made can be numerous for a complex project but may simply depend on whether the face (and the design ability) fits in the case of a small company requiring a letterhead. The face fitting is, however, an essential ingredient in any event. An identity programme can only develop successfully if the client is in constant and close contact with the consultant throughout and if mutual trust and empathy are absent during an eighteen-month project it is unlikely that the result will be either satisfactory or sympathetic to the company's ambitions.

Range of Expertise

The scale and range of abilities of the consultancy must match the requirements if the client is not to be obliged to co-ordinate a clutch of individual inputs. Even medium-sized corporate identity programmes cannot sensibly be handled by a one man band. In addition to a structured hierarchy of design talent, financial control, project management and production expertise are essential ingredients. Marketing, research and analysis skills can be obtained elsewhere but if provided by the consultancy a more integrated and cohesive result will undoubtedly be achieved.

Track Record

A consultancy's previous work is the immediately visible evidence of its suitability and is a persuasive factor; however it should not be assumed that if a consultancy's previous client list does not coincide with the project in hand that it will be unable to produce the optimum solution. Design is not portrait painting but a broadly based discipline which should be capable of crossing many borders. Conversely, if the solutions on show simply do not strike any chords, it would be pointless to proceed. Design

DESIGN WEEK

30 MARCH 1990 £1

THE TOP 100 DESIGN GROUPS

1990
SURVEY
OF
BRITAIN'S
BIGGEST
EMPLOYERS
AND
FEE EARNERS

The design industry is highly competitive and, perhaps understandably, image conscious. There are literally thousands of consultancies from which to choose ranging from one man bands to massive international conglomerates incorporating advertising, public relations, even behavioural psychologists. Some are design led, some marketing led, some research led.
A bewildering choice for a small or medium-sized company wishing to position itself in some meaningful way (the multinationals tend to consult the multinationals). At the bottom line, either the face fits or it doesn't.

solutions of any kind need to produce a positive if subjective response.

Facilities

Facilities and working environments communicate a great deal about any organisation - a design consultancy especially so, and it would be remiss for a client not to be exposed to his supplier's habitat. Perhaps most importantly, the consultant's attitude to the specific problem with which he is confronted will indicate his suitability or otherwise - albeit on a necessarily superficial level without the benefit of actually having been commissioned to proceed with the project.

The Shortlist

There are a variety of ways in which a shortlist can be constructed; bodies such as the Design Council or the Chartered Society of Designers can be consulted; organisations whose visual identities are to be admired can be contacted for information as to who has been responsible; alternatively golf partners and people at dinner parties invariably have suggestions (although this latter course tends to be less reliable).

The elements which constitute the design industry vary wildly in terms of size, standards, degrees of research as against pure design, management philosophies and methods of working and the comparison of like for like is not a simple matter.

Approach

The design industry as we know it may appear on the surface to be reasonably well established but when taken in the context of other twentieth century occupational phenomena, such as advertising or public relations, it has tended not to consolidate any predictable approach to the disciplines of the market-place. There are a variety of reasons for this, ranging from rapid changes in the market's expectations to the fact that there is little communality in the way in which most consultancies are constructed or managed.

A symbol for Business Sponsorship of the Arts. A block monogram treatment which avoids clumsiness.

The Specialists

With the increasing client demand that MBAs, market analysts and research experts should become as much part of the design process as the drawing boards, the industry is rapidly polarising into large multi-disciplinary units on the one hand and small 1960s-type 'hot shops' (who want no truck with such things) on the other. The middle ground is being squeezed, making it increasingly difficult to establish any new consultancies capable of handling corporate identity programmes. The majority of firms in this area are therefore well established - a fact that will doubtless reassure the faint-hearted when making their selection.

Extremities

The choice is wide; in extremis, a fat analytical report possibly resulting in a thin design solution might be set against an uninformed but intuitive stroke of genius; a bill for £1m for a new company structure or a face lift for £5k; pre-agreed fees or hourly charges, mark-ups on outside services or time charges for project management (or both) - the client will need to carefully weigh the options in order to achieve a dovetailed relationship.

THE APPOINTMENT

The logistics of selection would obviously be dictated by the individual company's management style. However, a great deal of management time wastage can be avoided if the process is structured in

Examples of a design consultancy's promotional literature aimed at potential clients, depicting completed projects.

operationally viable stages. A wide trawl of consultancies' own literature will provide an overall picture of the industry's capabilities, out of which three or four companies should emerge as being potentially viable. An outline brief can then be distributed to the candidates with a request for some written response as to how they would approach the project, in what time frame and in what cost parameters. This would form the basis for discussions with the consultancies, ideally at their studios, when they should be given the opportunity to give a further credentials presentation.

An alternative route is to finance the three or four consultancies to produce preliminary creative solutions from which to choose. However, there are disadvantages in this approach - an escalation of management time would be inevitable, as detailed briefing and consultations with each company would be obligatory if the solutions were to have any value and the cost of the initial indecision in terms of both time and fees can be considerable.

THE PATH TO SOLUTION

Once the appointment is made, whatever degree of research and project familiarisation is thought appropriate to the task should precede any creative work; the findings can focus and crystallise the original brief, but they can also distort it.

The creative path towards a solution can be tortuous if not carefully phased, with as much on-going contact as possible built into the process at strategic points. Discussions of initial ideas at an early stage can avoid expensive time being consumed in the wrong direction. The ability to 'read' a visual intention from a sketch is not a talent possessed by all, and the consultancy will need to make a judgement as to how explicit their early presentations should be in order to accurately communicate their ideas.

Interaction
Consultations and discussions on sketch stages should lead to a final exposition of the complete concept with minimal surprises. While it is unwise for earlier stages to be exposed to more than one or two designated key company personnel (too many cooks, design by committee, etc) it is both politic and in the future operationally imperative that the decision-makers in the company be exposed at the outset to the nature of the operation; without their support, implementation stages can be hampered or even sabotaged.

Objectivity
Adjustments will inevitably be suggested, but the chairman's wife displaying a preference for blue over green should not be a criterion on which to disrupt a scheme. The logic of the proposals should be examined; their relevance to the company and its markets, their operational feasibility and their

response value should be assessed, but a board of 20 directors voicing their individual subjective views requires control and nerve if the end result is not to be diluted to the point of disappearance.

An internal company magazine devoted to the launch of a new visual identity.

THE LAUNCH

Corporate identity can have a powerful and beneficial effect on staff morale (indeed, this factor is often the *raison d'être* of the exercise) and its launch to the company as a whole requires consideration if this advantage is not to be dissipated. A well-orchestrated presentation of the new or focused company values as illustrated by their translation into visual terms can lend impetus to creating the reality behind the image. Company loyalty can be enhanced at a stroke if the personality and purpose of the organisation are delineated in a way with which employees can identify. The distribution of a leaflet or brochure on the subject to all staff members, endorsed, or ideally, written by the chief executive can signal the seriousness with which management regards the exercise. If logistics permit, this can be enhanced by a joint presentation by management and the design consultants to all staff.

IMPLEMENTATION

The responsible and controlled implementation of an identity programme and its on-going management is crucial to maximising the advantages to be gained in the medium and long term and specific structures and liaison systems need to be put in place.

There are two possible avenues to be pursued: the gradual introduction of the scheme by amortisation of existing stocks of, say, stationery and forms or the Big Bang where as much as possible is changed at a given time. The former is cheaper, but lacks the impact necessary for maximising the public relations advantage while the latter requires more concentrated management time.

Although the tea lady's attitude to corporate culture is probably not germane to constructing a visual identity, she will nevertheless need to live with it. The involvement and commitment of top management to the introduction and maintenance of an identity programme is essential if the total staff are to be sympathetic to its aims and not sabotage, even through inattention, its central tenets.

Identity requires management input to the same or even greater degree than stock control or cash flow, and structures need to be put in place in order to ensure its efficiency.

The importance of the involvement of top management in the instigation and development of a visual identity programme cannot be over-estimated. The productive interaction of the consultancy with the client company should take place on a variety of levels - in the formulation of design policy, in the on-going implementation of the scheme and in its control.
The responsibility for design management should be vested in a dedicated individual within the company whose task it is to co-ordinate internal design requirements, control budgets and liaise with the consultancy and outside suppliers.

A well ordered management structure created specifically for the implementation of an identity scheme will ensure that the initial costs involved are not dissipated.

DESIGN MANAGEMENT

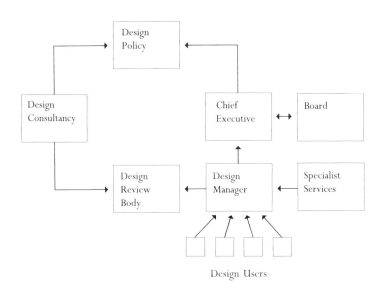

Design Users

115

DESIGN MANAGEMENT

Ideally the chief or a senior executive of the company will need to assume ultimate responsibility for the programme; it is essential that the authority of the company is perceived to be genuinely behind the project if it is to command the respect necessary for its implementation. His points of contact with the design consultancy should be on two levels; in the formulation of design policy and in periodic reviews convened to ensure that the policy is being correctly implemented. Additional management involvement is the appointment of a design manager whose essential role on a day to day basis is to co-ordinate design users' requirements and their production through the design consultancy or specialist services.

The Manual

He would also act as a filter - a guardian of the corporate identity principles. These principles would have been supplied by the design consultancy more often than not in the form of a design manual.
This document would set out specifications for the basic ingredients to be interpreted by design suppliers. Ideally this should be a flexible 'user-friendly' affair, capable of constant updating.
The massive and unalterable tomes produced for the identity programmes of the 1960s have served simply to ossify their message and therefore the appearance of their subject. An identity programme will sustain a longer life if its parameters allow for evolution.
The influence of stylistic changes in visual language

such as the fashionability of typefaces or colour will relegate an inflexible set of visual rules to obsolescence within a few years.

The design manual; the dead hand of stultifying authoritarianism if mis-conceived or misused. Visual perceptions and responses are ephemeral, subject to shifts in cultural mores. The ossification of an organisation's culture can be achieved at a stroke by encapsulating its ethos in the moment of time it takes to write the rules.These 1960s tomes still abound, numbing the minds of designers inheriting the rules and closing the minds of their employers to any relevant deviations. There are, of course, rules to be obeyed in order to maintain some continuity, some sense of continuing identity, but the visual stimuli to which we respond changes almost daily - dictated by more fast moving media than the design manual. A human manual - the consultant - is on the whole a better bet The CIMA manual, is calculated to establish only the basic and immutable rules.

REVIEW BODY

The management control mechanism is the establishment of a 'Design Review Body', meeting perhaps monthly, and consisting of the executive responsible for the programme, the design manager, representatives of the design consultancy and, on an *ad hoc* basis, those senior managers whose departments' use of design is under discussion. Individual projects should be reviewed retrospectively in order to maintain contact with the programme as a whole and wherever possible proposals for new projects should be approved.

The management of design has become a highly professional activity in its own right. An understanding of what design can achieve, the process by which it operates and how it can best be channelled in the interests of any given requirement are the essential ingredients.

CIMA's manual, a simple A4 publication, is regularly up-dated.

Basic instructions in a design manual are all that are necessary. An identity scheme will not move forward if stifled by too many design edicts.

Basic Copy and Layout Principles

Basic Layout Principles CIMA

A Summary

1. IDENTIFICATION OF NEED

- Represent and project a new company.
- Clarify relationships in an acquisition or merger.
- Signify new ownership (ie a management buy-out).
- Represent a shift in company function.
- Correct market perceptions.
- Motivate staff, improve morale.
- Raise profile.
- Increase competitiveness.
- Replace a dated or anachronistic image.
- Increase recruitment calibre.
- Focus market position.
- Rationalisation of brand/corporate images.

2. ESTABLISH OUTLINE BRIEF

- Analysis of current perceived problems.
- Identify eventual goal.
- Establish ball park budget.
- Estimate time scales.

3.   CONSULTANCY SHORTLIST

The outline brief can be submitted to:

- The Chartered Society of Designers (CSD), or
- The Design Council.

for recommendation for a shortlist of, say, three or four consultancies.

Otherwise those organisations for whom successful and comparable projects have been completed can be contacted for recommendations.

4.1 CHOICE OF CONSULTANCY/CREDENTIALS

Factors which need to be ascertained:

- Track record.
- Understanding of the brief.
- Understanding of the market in which the company operates.
- Understanding of the company's position in the market.
- Relative importance of the project to the consultancy.
- In-house facilities
  (ie artwork, desk top publishing, etc).
- Relationships with outside suppliers
  (ie printers).
- Scale of consultancy related to project.
- Quality of working environment.

120

- Client liaison structure.
- Calibre of the personnel allocated to the project.
- Charging methods.
- Personal rapport.

4.2 CHOICE OF CONSULTANCY/CREATIVE PITCH

An alternative, if somewhat expensive, route in terms of both management time and fees is to commission several consultants to arrive at a series of creative solutions from which to choose.

5. RESEARCH

In order to complement information contained in the initial brief and focus accurately on the exact nature of the project, the consultancy will need to carry out some research. The depth and extent of this stage will depend upon the complexity of the problem and the level of budget allocated.

Interviewees might include:

- Trade press.
- Company key staff.
- Company employees.
- Competitors.
- Clients/customers.
- Suppliers.

Knott, Michael, DES RCA MSIAD, Seaton Mill, Ickham, (
Knott, Simon, BA, 32 Burlish Crossing, Stourport-on
Knowles, Sandra Jane, BA(HONS), 6 The Parslins, Dee
Knox, Cameron, 10B Dickson Street, Hawick, Roxbur
Knox, Graham A, MSIAD, 16 Matford Lane, St Leonard
Knox, John, MSIAD, 65 Albert Road West, Bolton, Lanc
Knox, Kevin Nicholas, BA, 76 Halston Point, Balben F
Knuckey, Stephen, c/o 58 Arthur Road, Shirley, Sout
Kohli, Arun, 27 Furness Road, Fallowfield, Manchest
Koren, Vilhelm, DESRCA FSIAD, Flat 4, 62 Holland Park
Kovalainen, P H, 11 The Mall, Southgate, London N14
Kramer, David Ian, 'Stone House', Elmley Lovett, Dro
Krol, Stan, DA FSIAD, 7 Lowther Road, London, SW13 9
Kroll, Natasha, RDI FSIAD, 5 Ruvigny Gardens. London
Kunze, Stephen, BA, 152 Dukes Avenue, Ham, Richmo
Kurlansky, Mervyn, FSIAD, Pentagram, 61 North Whar
Kusmirek, Anthony, DIP AD MINSTM MSIAD, Poplar Farm
Kuzmicz, Karol, BA, 22 Meynell Close, Melton Mowbra
Kwan, Jeffrey, MSIAD, 131 Midhurst Road, London, W1:
Kyte, Nigel, BA, 1 Oakfields Road, London, NW11 0JA (
L'Estrange, B M, MSIAD, 29 Swallow Drive, Kensingtoı
Lacey, Bartus Mark, Bere Ern, Middle Assendon, Hen
Lacey, Glyn Mark, 4 The Greenway, Holly Tree Meadov
Lacey, Karen, Bere-Ern, Middle Assendon, Henley-or
Lacome, Myer, MSIAD, 72 Tay St, Newport On Tay, Fife,
Ladbrook, Sian Gale, BA(HONS), 141 Bennerley Road,
Lagden, S, MSIAD, 56 Homewood Avenue, Cuffley, Nr P
Lai, Wai Chu, Maldwyn House, Station Road, Llanrws
Laidler, Kenneth, MSIAD, 18 Summerhouse Farm, Eas
Laidler, Trevor, NDD MSIAD FRSA FSAI, 7 Princes Crescer
Lainchbury, Graham D M, MSIAD, 9B Tudor Road, Upp
Laing, Albert B, MSIAD, Caradoyne, Elm Bank Road, W
Laird, Michael D, OBE FSIAD, 22 Moray Place, Edinburʒ
Lake, David John, Sulgrave House, Queen Road, Croı
Lake, Ian R, 'Chez Nous', 44A Dorchester Road, Weyb
Lake, Susan M, 102 Coleraine Road, Blackheath, Lor
Lakhoo, Nazira, 53 Palmer Court, Shrewsbury Crescc
Lalau-Keraly, Catherine, 29D Colville Terrace, Londoı
Lam, Judy, 3 Croylands Drive, Surbiton, Surrey, KT6 6
Lamb, Thomas U, FSIAD, 209 Wingrove Rd, Fenham, N
Lambert, Bertram, 10 Grangecourt Road, Stamford F
Lambert, Claire, 17 Warkton Lane, Kettering, Northaı
Lambert, Elizabeth, BA, 8 Old Exeter Street. Chudleiʒ
Lee, Mary, 67 High Street, Dover, Kent, CT16 1EB (20
Lee, Maurice, FRIBA FSIAD ALI, 42 New Road, Digswell,
Lee, Patrick J, MSIAD, 10 Beaulieu Gdns, Winchmore F
Lee, R D, DIP ARCH RIBA FRSA MSIAS FRIAS AMBIM, 1A Chu
Lee, Robert A, MSIAD, 63 Cicada Road, London, SW18
Lee, Vernon Yew Koon, MSIAD, 10 Riverdale Road, Eas
Leech, Deborah, 12 Rock Grove, Kemp Town, Brightoı
Leech, Jon, BA(HONS), 47 The Strand, Fleetwood, Lanc
Legg, Richard Wilfred, Holly Tree Cottage, Gussage A
Leggett, Nicholas, 223 Oving Road, Chichester, West
Leggo, Andrew John, BA(HONS), 61D Bedford Road, Cl
Leigh, Christopher, 53 Winstanley Road, Sale, Chesh
Leigh, Patricia Barbara, 29 Longspring, Watford, He
Leigh, Peter, BA, 29 Longspring, Watford, Hertfordshi
Leigh, Raymond H, AA DIP ARIBA FSIA, 49 Pittville Lawn
Leith, Jake, MA, 'Heathfield', King George Avenue, Bu
Lelie, Herman, 23 Marylands Road, London, W9 2DN
Lemm, Elaine Mary, 153 Lower Mickletown, Methley, I
Lennard, Valerie, BA, The Cyphers, Brandon Court, Sl
Lennon, Adam, 42 Greenside, Slough, Berkshire (21S
Lennon, Dennis, MC FSIAD A FRIBA, 3 Fitzhardinge Stre
Leon, David, FSIAD, 3 Temple Station Buildings, Victo
Leonard, Jane, 24 Shaftesbury Road, Earlsdon, Cove
Leroy, Michael Andrew, 8 Ridgeway Crescent, Sunde
Leslie, Keith, MSIAD, 32 The Fairway, Sittingbourne, K
Lester, Graham, MSIAD, 138 Eskdale Avenue, Cheshaı
Lettice, Ian, Garden Flat, 20 Offerton Road, London,
Leung, March Siu Seung, 19 Malwood Road, London,
Leung, Nina, 131 Midhurst Road, London, W13 (734 5
Leung, Wendy Yuen-Tai, BA(HONS), 19 Hill View, Primrc
Levassor, G P, BA, 17 Ponsonby Terrace, London . . . .
Leveson-Gower, Catherine Anne, BA, 8B Wyfold Road,
Levick, Yvette, 1 Top Cottage, Upper Coberley, Nr Che
Levien, Robin Hugh, MSIAD, 10 Cloudesley Square, Isl
Levings, Christopher John, MSIAD, 264A Halley Road, I
Levingston, Norbert Yves, MSIAD, 79 Galba Court, Aug
Levy, Audrey, DES RCA FSIAD, 3 Brook Green Studios, D
Lewis, Alan Robert, 4 The Drive, Sheffield, S6 4AL (33
Lewis, Christopher, BA, 37 Ribblesdale Road, Streath
Lewis, Dennis R, ARWA MSIAD, Fords Creative Ltd, Towɛ
Lewis, Edward, 49 Fern Street, Cwmbwrla, Swansea,
Lewis, Gerard, 59 Tylecroft Road, London, SW 16 (01 ɛ
Lewis, Graham, FSIAD, Chief Designer Interior Design

Longley, Sandra, Flat 3, 13 Alexandra Road, Sale, Ch
Longshaw, Alison, 9 Agecroft Road East, Prestwich,
Longworth, Mark, 174 Mount Pleasant, Wembley, Mic
Lopez-Sagua, Sergio, BA, 14 Green Hillway, Shirley, S
Lord, Peter J, RIBA AADIPL(HONS) FSIAD, Austin-Smith-L
Lord, Richard Allan, MSIAD, 5 St Philips Street, Chelt
Los, Anna Maria, BA, 15 Mornington Street, Keighley,
Love, Lindsay Jean, Ozendyke Cottage, Ryther, near
Lovell, Frances Marian, 'Little Barn', Rodney Stoke,
Low, Leslie W, MSIAD, 3 Holland Road, Bath, Avon, BA
Lowder, Gary, 17 Chiltern Close, Cove, Farnborough,
Lowdon, Brian, The Heights, Hwrst Road, Hebden Br
Lowe, Andrew Peter, The Croft Hotel, Tenby, Dyfed, SA
Lowe, Beverley Ann, 5 Abney Court, Belmont Road, T
Lowe, J Roger, FSIAD NDD, Netherfield, Nether Street, F
Lowe, Richard S, BA, 126A Keighley Road, Skipton, N
Lowish, Kate Ann, BA, The Ruddings, Eastoft Road, L
Lowndes, Rosemary M, FSIAD, 132 Tachbrook Street, L
Lownsborough, Dilys Christine, MSIAD, Canberra, 33
Lowry, Patrick, MSIAD, Rock Cottage, Reigate Hill, Re
Lozano, Felix, 10 Crowhurst Lane, Sidley, Bexhill On
Lucantoni, Peter, 40 Brassey Road, Winchester, Ham
Lucas, J W, Shillington Manor, Hitchin, Herts (046 27
Lucas, Jonathan, 37 Nesburn Road, Sunderland, Tyn
Lucas, Paul, 616 Old Ford Road, London, E3 2JJ (01 9
Luck, Carole, 22 Oakfield Street, Roath, Cardiff . . .
Lucking, Norman Arthur, MSIAD, White House, Hilliard
Ludlow, Christopher, FSIAD, Henrion Ludlow & Schmid
Luff, Martin, BA, 124 Croxted Road, West Dulwich, Lo
Lukaszewicz, Barbara, BA, 9 Grosvenor Avenue, Kidd
Lumas, Whitney, 14 Carfax Close, Sidley, Bexhill on S
Lumby, Jane, 34 Abbeydale Grove, Leeds, LS5 3RE (L
Lumby, Neil John, Riversleigh Gate, The Hill, Langpo
Lumby, Stephen Richard, MSIAD, 9 Church Lane, Mell
Lumsden, Callum James, MA RCA MSIAD, 7 Thurleigh R
Lupton, Stephen Roy, 43 Hadfield Street, Walkley, Sh
Lupton, Tom, MA FSIAD, Orchard Close, Winterbrook, W
Lyall, W. Alison, 'The Little Neuk', Muckhart, Dollar C
Lyell, Nicholas, MSIAD, Lyemond Design Ltd, 12 Yeom
Lynam, Kenneth, Leybank, 8 Oast Road, Oxted, Surre
Lynch, Ann, FSIAD, 43 Sir Davids Park, Southborough,
Lynch, John J, MSIAD DA(EDIN) MBIID, 327 Lanark Road,
Lyne, Alan J, MSIAD, c/o Idp Consultants Ltd, PO Box 1
Lynn, Richard Jonathan, BA, 29 Graham Park Road,
Lyon, David S, FSIAD, 68 Weir Road, Kibworth Beauch
Lyon, Edward, MSIAD, 102 Silhill Hall Rd, Solihull, We
Lyon, James Alexander, 37 Montrose Avenue, Whitto
Lyon, Robert O, MSIAD, 35 West View Road, Keynsham
Lyons, Alan, 52 Coniston Road, Peterborough, Camb
MacKinnon, Mairi, 40 Keith Street, Stornway, Isle of
MacLeod, John, MSIAD, 2 Northumberland Street Lane
MacAsaet, Victoria, 5 Cygnet House, 184-194 Kings
MacBrayne, Duncan George, Barbican Y.M.C.A., Fan
MacDonald, Alastair, MSIAD, 9 Lyndhurst Gardens, GL
MacDonald, Alastair, 15 Foulstone Row, Wombwell, B
MacDonald, C Jane, MSIAD, Dell Cottage, Dog Kennel
MacDonald, Robert A, MSIAD, 82 Dernier Road, Tonbri
Mace, Steven, 12 Augusta Close, The Grove, Portland
MacGregor, Colin, FSIAD, Belvedere, The Dardy, Llang
MacHin, Alex K, 4 Holmsdale Road, South Darenth, D
MacHin, Jean, 43 Long Valley Road, Gillow Heath, Bic
MacHin, Michael F, 2 Sea View, Netley Abbey, Southa
MacKay, David Stewart, DA FSIAD, 57 Chiddingstone S
MacKay, W G, DA(EDIN) MSIAD, 3 Castle Street, Carlisle
MacKel, Sean, BAHONS, 3 Wolfhill Avenue South, Ligo
MacKender, Gary, 42 Halsall Avenue, Sheffield, S9 4J
MacKenzie, Ian T, MSIAD, Flat 58, St Johns Court, Finc
MacKenzie, Stuart Bernard, MSIAD, Tatlers Lane Cotta
MacKenzie-Kerr, Ian, ARCA MSIAD, 46 The Priory, Priory
MacKey, Catherine Monica, BA, 132A Park Hill Road,
MacKey, Ken, MA(RCA), 14 Harmood Street, Chalk Farr
Mackey, Margaret Roddick, 22 Dovecote Close, Coun
Marshall, Alan C, FSIAD, 45 Forefield Lane, Great Cros
Marshall, Elizabeth, 14A Fieldhouse Road, London, S
Marshall, Eric, FSIAD A M INSTM, Flat 8, 5 Carlton Gdns
Marshall, J C W, FSIAD, 50-56 Wharf Road, London, N1
Marshall, Karl Edward, 117 Whinney Hill Park, Brigho
Marshall, Leslie W, MSIAD, 33 Northfield Road, Blaby,
Marshall, Margo, BA(HONS), 25 Park Avenue, Dundee
Marshall, Roger, 87 Chessel Crescent, Bitterne, Sout
Marshall, Samuel, MSIAD, 21 Malden Hill, New Malden
Marshall, Stephen, Beacon Fold, 38 Elmers Green La
Marshall-Hilton, Stephen, MSIAD, 47 Main Road, Shirl
Marson, David William, BA, Design Department, BBC
Martin, A Ronald, SGA FRSA FSIAD, 16 Valverde House,
Martin, Alexander, 36 Hamilton Crescent, Brentwood

A balance between objective and subjective attitudes is essential if an accurately targeted solution is to be arrived at.

6. REPORT/BRIEF #2

Conclusions drawn from research will, after discussion with the company, result in a refined brief; a platform on which to build creative solutions.

7. CONCEPT PRESENTATION

Initial concept routes would be presented to the company for evaluation and response, the most appropriate being selected for development.

8. SOLUTION PRESENTATION

The chosen route would be refined and developed, its application being demonstrated on a number of relevant items such as stationery, advertising, vehicles and packaging.

9. IMPLEMENTATION

Establish liaison structure:

- Appoint internal manager with access to chief executive and control of budgets.
- Convene regular review body meetings.

Establish timetable geared to external/internal implementation and target date for the production of a control manual.

10. ON-GOING MAINTENANCE & DEVELOPMENT

Establish mechanisms whereby the scheme is under constant review as to its effectiveness and relevance to prevailing circumstances.

Basic Elements

The WH Smith design manual. A loose leaf update publication allowing maximum flexibility while providing immutable guidelines for the use of basic elements.

BASIC ELEMENTS
The Symbol
Outline Version

5 The same rules apply to the use of the outline version as for the solid version although its application is more limited. It has been developed for use on transparent surfaces such as windows, acetate packaging etc, where it is desirable to see through the symbol, and in instances such as some stationery items where it is desirable to have a light-weight symbol.
6 For sizes to be used in the outline version which are less than the smallest shown below, see overleaf.

BASIC ELEMENTS
The Symbol
Solid Version

1 The symbol is made up of three initial letters of the Company name, the S being dominant. It can be used in two forms: solid and outline and is designed to be used in conjunction with the logotype (see subsequent pages) with certain specific exceptions which are referred to in other sections. In no circumstances may the symbol be redrawn. The samples shown below and overleaf can be used as artwork, either same-size, reduced or enlarged.
2 The smallest practical size at which the standard version of the symbol can be used is shown at the bottom of this page. For sizes smaller than shown here, see overleaf.
3 With the exception of some rare examples for use in packaging and display the symbol must always be used in the upright position shown here.
4 The symbol can be reversed out of a solid background or used in the positive version, both shown below.

5 The Ingredients of Visual Identity

XEROX

A strange almost unpronounceable name which nevertheless has achieved a high degree of memorability, it being inculcated into our language as a description of its product. Hoover is another example, though few brand names have achieved this valuable marketing edge as it depends largely on being first in the field.

NOMENCLATURE

Next to the human element the perceived identity of any organisation depends first and foremost upon its name. Names can be succinct, memorable, capable of easy verbalisation and visualisation and produce relevant responses. On the other hand, usually due to having been established without consideration of their marketing value, they can be unsympathetic, unmemorable and on occasions just misleading.

The requirements of new name generation are always unique, ranging from the adjustment of long established trading names to the creation of an entirely new brand; or from the consolidation of a group of merged or acquired companies, to the replacement of a name which, through changed trading conditions, has become irrelevant.

New name generation requires specialist research and literary skills. Furthermore, nomenclature is an emotive subject: family names have sentimental attachments; the loss of personal profile, or simply the loyalty/comfort factor can impinge on a rational market oriented solution. The combination of logical research and sympathetic politics can ensure the successful outcome of a nomenclature project.

With the massive proliferation of individual companies over the past 50 years, registerable names which fulfil identity or marketing requirements are becoming exceedingly difficult to source. In the US, this has resulted in heavy reliance being placed on computer generated names - abstract bits and pieces of supposedly emotive words stitched together into what often results in a sterile and unmemorable handle. Witness the metamorphosis from United Airlines to Allegis.

Acronyms are often considered to be an easy way out of the problem, but examples such as GMBATU, cited earlier in this book, have a sonority which resembles the name of an African village; EETPU, another union, is simply impossible to verbalise without resorting to a media invention in order to circumvent the problem: 'double e-tee-pee-you'.

Good use of acronyms is by no means impossible; ASH (Action on Smoking and Health) has the double virtue of being both descriptive and pronounceable. ICI has sufficient exposure and sonority to sustain it, as does BBC and for that matter GMB.

Ponderous and authoritarian names such as Imperial Chemical Industries or the British Broadcasting Corporation are best forgotten (and usually are). Their replacement by initial letters enables the designer to inject some accessibility into the visual presentation of the organisation concerned.

Rockefeller, Rothschild, Morgan, Lever - all organisations still for better or worse imbued with the character of their founders. The names reek of dynastic solidity - an undeniable advantage in today's volatile big business climate.

Probably the worst results are constructed from the company founders' initials; doubtless a satisfactory ego massage, but with little or no chance of market or cultural relevance. M&G for example, although one of the largest financial services companies in the UK, has little or no value as a name. Furthermore, its sterility is not rejuvenated by proclaiming itself a member of organisations rejoicing in the additionally enigmatic nomenclature of IMRO and LAUTRO.

Birds, animals and fish carry emotive connotations which can be utilised to express certain company characteristics, though care must be exercised that the connotations are not misinterpreted; 'shark' for an accountant would be unfortunate, as would 'sparrow' for a bulldozer manufacturer.

Unfortunately for those consultancies now seeking to mine this potentially productive seam, most of the animal species have already been devoured and secure registration has become a major difficulty, as borne out by the Kingfisher furore; when Woolworth, in the interest of signalling change and consolidation, decided to create a holding company encompassing all its operations - from DIY superstores to its traditional high street operation. The Kingfisher name was chosen to herald the new image. This move was rewarded by a queue of litigants suing the company for plagiarism.

However, those anthropomorphic appellations which have successfully been snapped up have proved their

worth; Caterpillar, Cow and Gate, Camel (on the surface a dubious notion), et al are all now unavailable.

The personalisation of a company is no bad thing: the notion that there is an individual in charge, however remote (and sometimes in fact dead) does nevertheless lend an aura of accessibility - Rockefeller, Morgan, Rothschild or Taylor Woodrow all elicit a more human response than, say, Xerox or JCB.

Established names which sprang from some long forgotten and now radically changed circumstances should not automatically become subject to replacement. A certain quaintness, not necessarily a minus in some circumstances, surrounds such organisations as Save and Prosper. There is a human element here with which it is possible to identify. It is also the case that some of the more ludicrous and inappropriate names become so embedded in the social psyche that their actual meaning becomes sublimated to their recognition value. In order to qualify for an insurance policy, few would now assume that to have had a bereavement in Glasgow was a prerequisite to consulting Scottish Widows for a pension scheme. On the other hand, quaintness can be manufactured; food products such as Mr Kipling, Colonel Sanders or Wendy's hamburgers are deliberate forays into gnomeland but no less effective, in terms of their market, for that.

The use of fictitious or at least human exaggerated characters in nomenclature can attribute instant tradition to a company or product. Mr Kipling and Colonel Sanders (who was in fact the genuine founder), though of different nationalities, both bestow their original and probably secret recipes on a grateful public. The human element, even if a trifle bogus, has great appeal.

Animals and birds are much used motifs both in nomenclature and visual terms. Anthropomorphic attributes can be read into their perceived behaviour, adding a further dimension to an organisation's character or function. Complicated jokes can be constructed around such devices - Fox's glacier mints represented by a polar bear or a delivery company calling itself Lynx. Camel, on the other hand, does not signal that the taste of its cigarettes would be particularly agreeable.

A more cynical attitude to nomenclature is the current paradoxical trend to signal a national origin which is perceived to be pre-eminent in its field without a product or service necessarily emanating from that area. Japanese technology was, until ten years ago, considered to be plagiaristic and therefore second-rate. The West now perceives that same technology as being in many ways superior to that of its original inspiration: imaginary Japanese names are now constructed for products which are, for example, manufactured in Holland and sold (usually under an 'own brand' label) in the UK.

On examination this deception is usually transparent, but the consumer is generally not over zealous in verifying authenticity if the product visually matches the promise. Dixon's Saisho brand is a case in point.

The degradation of original names is often a pragmatic but in marketing terms unsatisfactory resolution of a corporate nomenclature problem. Pacific and Orient, a powerful company whose original success depended upon the expansion of early 20th century shipping, eventually became a holding company concerned with a raft of activities ranging from general transport to building, construction and even vending machines. Through lack of decision at a certain point in its development it was obliged to anonymise its name to P&O, avoiding a misnomer but missing the opportunity to positively declare its function and intention. Any discernible character which could be ascribed to the company now therefore relies on a visual device (curiously, under the circumstances, a marine flag) which on its own achieves little in signalling its multi-function character. By a similar token, though perhaps in a more sinister vein, British and American Tobacco has succeeded in diminishing its name to BAT, thereby removing reference to the offending weed but unintentionally creating mental images of flying rodents.

The adoption of a colloquial usage can often be exploited in order to connect with the market on a more human level; 'NatWest' is certainly a more accessible name than the 'National Westminster Bank Plc'. The erstwhile Greater London Council was rarely referred to in terms other than 'the GLC'. 'The Pru', though not exploited by its comparatively recent corporate identity humanisation programme, might well have been an avenue to explore in terms of nomenclature.

Some names have never been understood, but exist because of their familiarity through exposure. TSB, ICI, TI etc are all organisations of which people are aware, but their culture and personality has to be portrayed by means other than their name; an expensive business, as carefully crafted and imaginative visual exposure is necessary to establish a sterile acronym on the public conscience. Names need to be memorable, descriptive, sonorous, emotive, capable of verbalisation and visualisation and above all appropriate.

NatWest

NatWest, The Pru,The Beeb, Woolies, Marks are all affectionate verbal reductions, curiously never translated into visual terms. NatWest however have exploited this phenomenon in the interests of appearing more human and accessible, although the heavy-handed typeface employed does tend to contradict the intention.

THE ADJUSTED NAME

It is often feasible to adjust existing names in order to more accurately fulfil the needs of changing circumstances - be it the culture of the company itself or its markets.

Bowes & Bowes Books

Although an established book shop when acquired by WH Smith, Bowes and Bowes had a somewhat lacklustre image which required a more elegant typographic treatment than hitherto. The addition of 'Books' and the ampersand was partly dictated by visual considerations - an example of an integrated design/nomenclature approach.

Hotels Plus

A chain of booking agents installed in all BAA airports, originally trading under 'Hotel Reservations'. The name was shortened to a more succinct statement which accurately reflected the broader offer (all business booking requirements were catered for). An additional requirement was to express the notion of its quick, efficient service.

Moonen Custom

Moonen Scheepfswerf NV, a Dutch boat builder selling a standard product mostly to its domestic market, decided to enlarge its boat yard capacity and create an entirely custom built product for the high net worth international customer. The combination of replacing the Dutch suffix with an internationally descriptive word and illustrating its product flexibility launched the company into a successful new era.

Next

Following the establishment of the first Next chain, the company commissioned an entirely new concept for the male market. The starting point was the name itself. Next had to be retained, but the male aspect of the offer needed to be expressed with originality, creativity and style. The addition of an M - Next to the power of men - was sufficient to achieve differentiation while visually transmitting the message. This chain became the benchmark for men's clothes retailing and one of the most successful in the group.

WH Smith

An important ingredient in the original WH Smith corporate identity programme was the recommendation to shorten its trading name - originally W. H. Smith and Son - to the simpler visual and verbal statement which has become one of the best-known and easily recognisable companies in the UK.

THE NEW NAME

The creation of brand new names for new ventures is generally a more difficult proposition for the aforementioned reasons - difficulty of registration or even accidental duplication.

Aquilla

The Sarova Group had decided to create a luxury health club in one of its hotels - The Rembrandt - with an interior designed to reflect the splendours of Rome. The brief, in addition to creating a graphic identity, was to source a name which accurately reflected this intention.

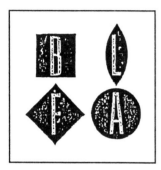

BLFA

A Ward White/Focus Shoes project to create a radical niche market offer for teenage shoes. However, the brief was broader than the creation of just another shoe shop. The requirement was to create specific merchandise areas which contained a wide variety of associated products. The name was generated by the initial letters of Basic (everyday, work) Leisure (after work, weekends) Flash (parties) and Action (sports).

Landmark

Another Ward White/Focus Shoe project, contrasting dramatically with BLFA, directed at the ABC1 market. The *double entendre* inherent in the name was a particularly strong starting point for the overall scheme.

Bridges

A restaurant on the Thames. The ambiguity of it being both an individual's name and a feature of the location created an intriguing solution.

Jo Gilbert's Voice Overs!
A small agency dealing with the supply of suitable
actors for 'unseen' voices dubbed on to commercials.
The protagonist's name was used as a prefix due to
her reputation within the industry. The use of the
exclamation mark within the name stemmed from the
visual 'comic strip' concept.

Reading Matters
The Early Learning Centre decided in 1988 to
establish a chain of outlets dedicated to children's
books, catering for the 0-12 age group.
The nomenclature exercise, pivotal to the development
of the concept, culminated in a solution which is both
intriguing, descriptive and memorable.

Shortstop
British Airports Authority commissioned a thematic
treatment, starting with a name, for a large restaurant
area at Gatwick Airport. The food was American,
the service fast. The solution caught the imagination of
thousands of bored passengers.

Snapshot
Snapshot stationery was developed as a brand name
for a new unique product range of greetings cards and
frames that incorporated personal photographs.

Vessel Du Vin

Importers of high quality wines. The brief was to create a name which firmly placed the company at the exclusive end of the market with a promise which would fulfil expectations.

The great names are often considered so because we know them through constant exposure - Shell, Mercedes-Benz and Xerox, but some, such as Jaguar, Caterpillar and Bell Telephone have an aptness and an emotive quality which successfully conjure up the function and the ethos of their subject. There are not many of these remaining to new companies, but to resort to computers to generate nomenclature must represent the thin edge of the wedge.

LOGOTYPE - THE VISUALISATION OF A NAME

Typography is in itself a formidable subject, starting as it does with hieroglyphics leading through to stone carved letters, Gutenberg's invention of moveable type, the great early twentieth century typographers such as Eric Gill up to present day computer generated digitised letter forms.

Perfectly straightforward and accepted typeforms, when 'doctored' to express some aspect of their activities, can achieve individuality.

The choice of style, of emotive quality and legibility is immense. Add the possibilities of computer distortion techniques, and the options are almost without limit. However, in order to obtain the exact form required to accurately reflect the designer's intention, most logotypes of note are in fact hand

136

drawn - or at least in some way altered from an available original typeface.

The way in which a company brand name appears is of crucial importance in terms of market perception. Anonymous typography requires further visual support, as in the case of Shell or NatWest, both of whom rely heavily on the use of symbols in order to establish their identities. Boots or Harrods on the other hand, has no need of such devices as the appearance of the names themselves has sufficient distinction and individuality to create instant recognition and recall.

Interestingly, it is often only names which are 'handwritten' which are capable of standing alone. Kellog's, St Michael and Cadbury are examples. The reason for this may be that to inject individuality into recognisable typography can lead to a somewhat tortured result. There are, of course, notable exceptions: ESPRIT the international fashion chain, CANTON the German electronics company, or NASA the American space agency are all examples of judicious juggling with accepted letter forms which achieve expressive individuality without tipping into the illegible or the bizarre.

The immediacy and uniqueness of a handwritten logotype are advantages which can in certain circumstances be exploited in the interests of expressing the personality of a company. The notion

ESPRIT, a visually stylish solution for a chain of fashion shops which only just avoids illegibility. Perhaps this kind of risk is worth it if it contributes to memorability. Having to work a bit for comprehension does little harm so long as the effort is rewarding. Designed by Tamotsu Yagi.

The manipulation of relatively conventional typography can be both expressive and visually compelling. CANTON produces hi-fi equipment; the notion behind the logotype is the expression of 'piano' through 'crescendo' to 'forte-fortissimo'. This works well in context, but in isolation could apply to many things. Designed by Christof Gassner.

NASA, the American space agency, launched its visual identity in 1974. Its stated intention was to express 'unity, technological precision, thrust and orientation towards the future', although this does sound a trifle like post-rationalisation. The device, however, works sufficiently well without the explanation. Designed by Danne & Blackburn Inc.

Actual signatures used for company names, short of using photographs of the protagonists, is as near as one can get to 'the personal touch'. Whether or not this is a desirable route depends on the nature of the business involved - it is unlikely that a large manufacturing company would benefit from such a ploy.

of using the main protagonist's 'signature' to represent a company bearing his name will communicate a personal ethos appropriate to a small organisation. 'Weiss' is an exclusive gallery dealing in rare and expensive antiques - the signature, employed as part of its corporate identity, implies the personal involvement of the owner. For a design consultancy, the use of the two founders' signatures implies that their creative input has not been diminished by the burden of management. Craftsmith, a chain of shops owned by WH Smith which dealt with craft oriented leisure activities is expressed by the use of a calligraphic, but nevertheless free, form of treatment.

Handwriting of a different kind - a less personal semi-calligraphic approach - can imply a craft oriented activity. The danger to be avoided in this instance is that the treatment should not appear too precious or esoteric if to be applied to a largish operation.

There are certain characteristics of typography which, through association communicate character, function or personality. The Times newspaper has a tradition which exudes respectability and reliability. Its typeface (not unreasonably called 'Times') has taken on the psychological aura of its namesake. 'Wanted' posters from the Wild West were printed with large block serif wood carved letters, later to be used for Western-film-type sequences. This type, if substituted for, say, the 'Times' based logotype of WH Smith would herald a totally different offer, and one which would in perceptual terms contradict the intended ethos of the company.

138

WHSMITH

W.H.SMITH

Typography is highly emotive and can, through association, elicit an infinite variety of responses - some right, some wrong.

Flowing script for a stationery company, digitised type for a computer company, stencilled type for an export company or italic type for a transport company are all obvious routes to be considered for the construction of a logotype; however other factors often interfere with logic - fashion being pre-eminent.

The typography used for UK motorway signage is designed to be highly legible, but is devoid of any emotional content. A company wishing to employ this family of letterforms for its name will therefore be in danger of projecting a somewhat sterile image. In the 1960s, this particular type and those from which it was derived, the Swiss typefaces Helvetica and Univers, were much in vogue and, with hindsight, were an unfortunate choice by such organisations as the National Westminster Bank.

abcdefghijklmnopqrstuvwxyz
ABCDEFGHIJKLMNOPQRSTUVWXYZ
1234567890.,-:;–!?()ß&£$

The 1960s Helvetica typeface. Arid or aggressive visual statements, often the result of a desire to mimic the prevalent graphic style of the time can in the long term become counter-productive. Fashion is by nature transitory, and should be regarded as such if durable visual identity expressions are to be resolved.

139

THE SYMBOL

As intimated earlier the symbol can be the visual encapsulation of the corporate intention; a powerful communicator of the visual message - the new heraldry, the visible icon, the fulcrum around which a visual identity can be constructed, though it is by no means an essential ingredient if other elements are orchestrated in a persuasive and compelling manner.

In this century, we have moved from American whimsy to Swiss austerity and from imagery derived from pop art to poor imitations of Matisse brush strokes, and have now arrived at something of a watershed.

Saul Bass' luminous globe.

Initial letters tortured into graphic shapes, monograms with anthropomorphic connotations, private abstract doodles and arrows sprouting in all directions characterise an alarming proportion of current identity programmes. There are notable and celebrated exceptions: Michael Wolff's goldfish for Addison Design fulfils every criteria; its beauty speaks for itself in an international language which requires no translation. Chermayeff and Geismar's Rockefeller Centre device has an elegant and classic simplicity which is both descriptive and compelling. Saul Bass' AT&T illuminated globe achieves a reassuring solidity while retaining its luminous quality, even in black and white.

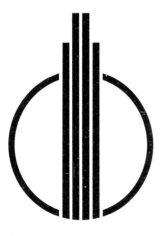

Chemayeff and Geismars' interpretation of a building.

Given the sophisticated reproduction techniques now available, it is becoming a somewhat less essential

140

A fish (by Michael Wolff), a building, a head - three-dimensional, illusory and relief. Illustrative, abstact, graphic/representational, - a design consultancy,The Globe Playhouse Trust, a health club. The techniques are interchangeable and only seem apposite because they have been used in these particular instances. A full colour detailed rendering of the building or a graphic/representational fish would be accepted for what they are - although the designers might also need to be interchanged.

Humour or at least levity can be an appropriate means of communication although perhaps not for a funeral parlour.

prerequisite that corporate identity elements should be capable of being reproduced in monochrome. However, newspaper advertising in colour is still extremely expensive, and not always available; a device which only communicates satisfactorily in full colour should still generally be avoided.

Humour was an element much exploited in early American marks of the twenties and thirties, but is now rarely seen. Most contemporary symbols are lacking in levity and have tended to take themselves too seriously. Humanity - the emotional response - is an ingredient not to be ignored on any level of communication. Smith and Milton's Van Blanc and Van Rouge for Citroen cars manage to catch the right note for a manufacturer who has always regarded its 2CV with amused tolerance. Pentagram's classic 'Goods and Chattels', launched in the 1960s, injected an appropriate fun element by the interchangeability of various artifacts either side of an ampersand. Apple Computers' multi-coloured apple with a bite out of it (get it?) is a nice touch, as is the 'r' dropping off the Reject Shop's matrix.

The human element however requires a focus - a positive reason. When considering how best to encapsulate the theme of an exhibition on Prince Albert, it became evident that general perceptions of his character and achievements were based on the sociological mores of Victorian England, largely dictated by the Queen after his early and untimely

To feel good about something is to identify with it. Tabro Sparkplugs, circa 1920, with a delightful depiction of an electrical charge; The Reject Shop, Van Rouge, and Apple all employ contemporary versions of both literary and visual puns, while Pentagram's Goods & Chattels interchangeable logos provide infinite variety and stimulation. Perhaps the bravest is Apple, it being the most unexpected in terms of its computer based business.

death. As the theme of the exhibition was to dispel this notion and illustrate his wide-ranging and innovative contribution to British industry, his encouragement of the arts and his love of social life (albeit somewhat thwarted by the governments of the day), a free form and unstuffy approach seemed apposite; a sketch portrait, apparently dashed off on the spur of the moment surmounting his fluid and immediate signature, communicated a more outgoing and creative ethos than might have been expected while his stance and expression retained the degree of dignity appropriate to his office.

Although not always appropriate, figurative devices are easier images with which to identify than abstract intellectualisations. The requirement for Britain's symbol for EXPO92 in Seville was to unequivocally express on the one hand nationality and on the other a determination to look to the future. The one single image which the world understands to be Great Britain is the union flag. Clichés of this kind should not necessarily be avoided if they possess instant recognition value and are at the same time capable of manipulation into another layer of communication. The striding figure emerging from its background needs no caption to be understood, even by the Cantonese. Likewise, Pentagram's symbol for a British Week in New York well illustrates the fact that versatility and originality can be injected into images which are not in themselves original.

BRITAIN
AT
EXPO '92

1930s

Inevitably, the prevalent visual culture, whether influenced by fine art, pop music or Swiss typography must to some extent influence the way in which visual identity components are conceived. There are few identity schemes which have not been evolved into contemporary relevance which can not be accurately dated.

1940s

1950s

1960s

North Sea Navigation, a shipping company; something, perhaps, about the high seas.

Ginger Group; a group of hairdressing salons.

Sterling; a construction company.

Information technology; introduced at the time when VDUs where proliferating.

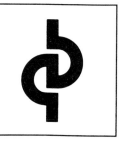

Guinness/Button; representing two equal partners in a financial consultancy.

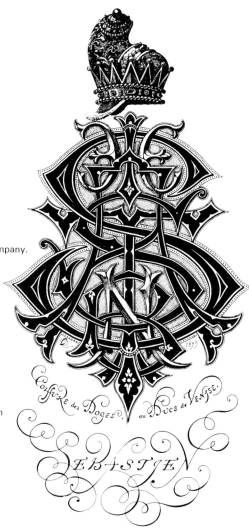

MONOGRAMS

The monogram as a personal device was developed in the nineteenth century by aspirants to heraldic status. Personalised dinner services, handkerchiefs, slippers and latterly car doors and tailor-made shirts were all emblazoned with the family patriarch's initials - a precursor of the current obsession with branding everything from T-shirts to running shoes.

The genre has since found its way into the visual vocabulary of commerce and industry and if manipulated expressively can be an effective and communicative device on which to build an identity.

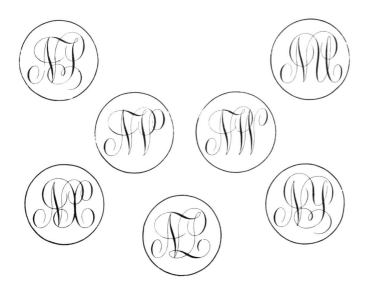

The design of monograms is the one graphic exercise on which everyone is a practised expert. Doodles on blotters, in school text books and telephone note pads; carved into trees or chalked on to walls - we all had a go.

The Doges of Venice were experts, as were the English Victorians, in developing these family devices in the absence of a granted coat of arms.

In contemporary visual identity programmes they are much used, their success however depending on whether they are able to express more than the purely aesthetic juxtaposition of letter forms.

Three disparate symbol treatments; for a festival of double bass music, for a festival devoted to Shaw and Elgar and for a development company concerned with buildings in London.

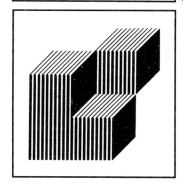

Two diverse architectural forms expressed in the same visual vernacular; one for an English estate agent, the other for a school of Islamic architecture. An illustrative but abstract symbol for the Queen Elizabeth Country Park, an area of two hills bisected by a road.

148

ILLUSTRATIVE SYMBOLISM

Illustration is perhaps the most direct method of depicting an object or a situation, but it is not simply the style of execution but the choice of subject which will determine its communicative value. American symbols of the twenties and thirties relied heavily on this approach, partly because the graphic designer as such had not yet appeared on the scene and it was therefore largely poster artists who were commissioned to produce visual representations of the company ethos.

A resurgence of this approach was marked by Michael Wolff's hummingbird for Bovis in the early 1970s - an unexpected and entirely successful exercise in changing people's perception of the building industry. His goldfish for Addison, another oblique visual reference, continues the tradition. London Wildlife's

Flora and fauna lend themselves particularly to illustrative treatments of visual identities, whereas less animate objects tend to be better treated by abstraction.

London Wildlife Trust

FALCON CONSTRUCTION

THE
TASTE CREATIONS
COMPANY

urban fox caught perhaps in the headlights of a car, London Zoo's one hundred and fiftieth anniversary symbol or Taste Creation's luscious cherry represent more literal approaches to the genre.

The solution to London's Theatre Museum identity relies entirely on illustration. The requirement was to communicate the breadth of activities covered by the museum within the performing arts - from film to circus and from classical theatre to contemporary comedy. The basic scheme consists of figures representing this spectrum parading across a stage. The idea is however extremely flexible, in so far as the stage motif can also be used for specific promotions or as a signing device - the title of an exhibition can for example appear on the stage, or directional arrows masquerade as scenery.

Illustration by definition stands a greater chance of international comprehension than the monogram or the captioned geometric abstract. Technically, however, it can present some difficulties in terms of reproduction - a finely executed full colour painting will obviously not be at its best if printed in a monochrome newspaper, and there are instances where a more formalised treatment is more appropriate.

NATIONAL MUSEUM OF THE PERFORMING ARTS

The squeezed citrus fruit device for Frulimpo, an Argentinian fruit juice export company, needed such diverse applications as stationery, packaging and stencilled wooden packing cases.

Its blocked shape simplicity was therefore an essential illustrative treatment dictated by technical requirements. In another instance, the record label for Cockerell Records needed a clear defined shape in which to insert typography - the eye being the boss hole at the centre of the record.

The 1930s had no inhibitions about using popular illustration styles to represent products or services. The resultant forceful and emotive images have their descendants in such notions as the Colonel Saunders benign face peering out from above his fried chicken emporia.

A contemporary ballet company's image, calculated to express their collective energy and verve.

The combination of logotype and symbol; the National Gallery and Chelsea Girl are perhaps uneasy bedfellows but the integration of their names into visual images shares a common approach.

THE COMBINATION

If two basic graphic elements are considered a necessary combination in order to more fully express the personality and purpose of an organisation - a logotype and a symbol - they need not only to be sympathetic, but in some instances indivisible.

In the extreme, the symbolic nature of an identity can be part of the name, as in the devices for the National Gallery or Chelsea Girl - two very different organisations requiring opposite modes of expression - established tradition as opposed to trendy fashion - but both designed with a similar structural approach.

The logotype can be a caption as in the case of The Marbella Tennis Club or the visual device can be the caption as in the identity statement for Benn Publishers. The Pasta Factory or EFTA on the other hand, employs a technique whereby the symbol is the logotype.

It is the particular and individual requirements of an identity which will dictate the structural approach to the use of the visual elements. In the case of the Arts Council, its main requirement was one of endorsement. Its client organisations such as The Royal Opera or the National Theatre possess their own distinctive identities and their own publicity material. In order to avoid a visual cacophony of conflicting identities and to minimise intrusion on the design intention of the variously produced posters, leaflets and general print, a solution was devised whereby a specific

Likewise a tennis club and a publisher are disparate entities, but the underline combination, one as logotype one as image, represent similar juxtapositions.

The Pasta Factory and the precursor of the common market share the technique of the image being the logotype.

position was decreed for the endorsement motif - a five-line stave device in the form of an A with the hint of a C - which by always being placed in the bottom right hand corner of all and any material caused minimum interference with a wide diversity of designs while at the same time strongly signalling the Arts Council's involvement.

Initially, the Arts Council's name was attached to the symbol, following the diagonal nature of the device. When familiarity with the device was established, the typography was removed and embodied in the overall design in whatever type style was appropriate.

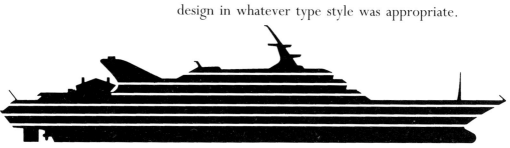

A symbol for the King of Saudi Arabia's yacht, the brief being to express its size and complexity.

Examples of relatively minor visual devices being added to the basic logotype in order to individualise and explain some aspect of the organisation. Hampers, a baker/restaurant; Thesis, an international consultancy; Jersey Island Plan, run by the official council.

A flexible approach to the relationship between symbol and logotype which relied on a build-up of exposure.

There are instances when from the outset the two elements need to be employed independently, but without jeopardising the overall identity.

The W H Smith identity was designed specifically to operate on two perceptual levels - the cube symbol being a 'stamp of ownership' for the core retail business while the logotype was designed to work on a raft of diverse endorsements.

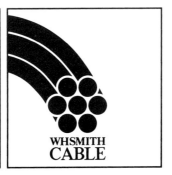

The shift in emphasis between visual elements can be dictated by market considerations. The WH Smith logotype when attached to the cube symbol represents its core High Street retail business. The logotype when detached and integrated in a secondary way with the visual components of its DIY business becomes an endorsement, lending credibility to the concept and positioning the operation slightly up-market from its competitors. When used in conjunction with a dominant symbol and descriptive name of a non-retail offer, it simply denotes ownership.

Now that the DIY operation is established, the WH Smith endorsement is no longer necessary and can therefore be easily detached from the visual identity.

Typography which complements or counterpoints the image. The Lamborghini bull is in a sense italic, as is the type. Mitsukiku, a chain of Japanese shops, is represented by an adaptation of a traditional Japanese symbol; the temptation to over-lard the message with brush stroke lettering was mercifully resisted.

A visual synergy between the elements can be as appropriate in given circumstances as a visual counterpoint. The type employed for Lamborghini is calculated to echo the 'italic' force of the bull above it, while Mitsukiku, a chain of shops in the UK selling imported Japanese merchandise, is deliberately Western in character, captioning as it does a Japanese- style motif.

PASTICHE

Pastiche: 'a work of art in the style of another artist', says the dictionary. It might also add, from another era. The notion of borrowing stylistic statements in order to express particular attributes can be an emotive and compelling means of visual communication.

The John Smith's corporate symbol deliberately delves into the past for its visual components. The brewery until comparatively recently traded under the 'Courage' banner; with pressure and an effective public relations campaign, CAMRA, an organisation dedicated to the promotion of real ale (and by implication the derogation of beer produced by the major brewers) forced the industry to re-examine the way in which its products were marketed. It was decided therefore to revive some of the original small brewery names which had previously been absorbed by the major players. The 'new' identity for John Smith's employs a re-drawn version of its original magnet symbol supported by typography of the time.

Images borrowed from heraldry can imbue an identity with a certain authority. Both the Lex Gold Shield and the Chantry Way devices, though treated in a contemporary fashion, have their roots in another time.

Pastiche, a difficult and often misunderstood direction to be taken when approaching either the re-visualisation of an established organisation or, perhaps more especially, a new one.

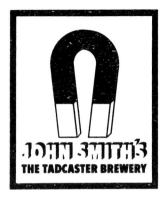

LEX
GOLDSHIELD

John Smith's image is a re-assemblage of various visual devices in use in the early part of this century, contemporary style being injected by the use of colour, juxtaposition and re-drawn type. In order to re-establish traditional values and at the same time remain visually relevant to the marketplace it is an appropriate use of pastiche.

THE CHANTRY CENTRE

Lex Goldshield and The Chantry Centre, a new vehicle leasing operation and a new shopping centre respectively, both employ pastiche of heraldry - that is to say, a totally contemporary skewing of a passé vernacular.

The age of traditional heraldry is passed. How therefore to depict the Silver Jubilee? Officialdom, the essence of Royal Patronage in a contemporary vernacular? We live for better or worse in a monarchical society, we respect the Crown - foreigners respect the Crown - the Crown respects the Crown.

But certain institutions or events need to communicate immediacy and relevance to contemporary mores while at the same time attaching Royal Patronage in some form. Rather in the same way that the Union Jack flag is the most cogent visual distillation of Britain, some graphic representation of a crown is the only immediately recognisable symbol of the monarchy.

The 1977 Celebrations of the Queen's Silver Jubilee, commissioned by a consortium representing London as distinct from Britain as a whole, wished to signal the City's particular and individual commitment to the event. Two clichés married into a single visual statement - St Paul's Cathedral integrated into the crown - formed the focus for a week's communal celebrations. The device was hand-painted onto pub doors, stencilled on to roadways, cast in bronze pavement plaques, emblazoned on to flags, depicted by flower planting in parks, printed on to funny hats, used on building hoardings, silk screened on to silver buses, used three dimensionally on walkway markers, decorated signing systems, respectabilised litter bins, and appeared on countless more-or-less decent souvenirs ranging from mugs to matchboxes. In a sense, the device had no 'corporate identity' control whatsoever, but succeeded in encapsulating Londoners' enthusiasm for the event, it being adopted by all and sundry in a bewildering, diverse array of applications. A visual pivot around which do-it-yourself expression of celebratory social cohesion was achieved - albeit momentarily.

OFFICIALDOM

Officialdom in any form is often stubbornly represented by coats of arms or heraldic devices of one kind or another. From local authorities to government departments, from professional bodies to royalty itself. There are, however, ways in which elements of this visual discipline can be abstracted and translated into a more contemporary visual idiom.

The symbol for the Queen's Silver Jubilee London Celebrations was designed for the widest possible application - it was stencilled on to roadways and hoardings - it was depicted in park flowerbeds - it was used on flags, on brochures, on signing systems and still in fact exists embedded in cast bronze in pavements throughout London, delineating a tourist walkway; any kind of heraldic visual treatment would have precluded its use in many of these situations although its inspiration derives from the heraldic vernacular.

The Bath city symbol likewise is a derivative of its original crown and shield, while the symbol for its event 'Monarchy 1000' translates the years into jewels without resorting to any over-literal or heraldic statement.

The Jubilee Tourist Centre; although part of the overall Jubilee celebrations needed to be perceived as a separate commercial enterprise.

'Monarchy 1000', an event staged in Bath to celebrate King Edgar's claim to be the first truly British monarch. Historians may dispute this as being a somewhat specious notion; however, he was enthroned in Bath, and it seemed a reasonable idea for Bath City Council to exploit the event.

A device depicting five crowns; a discarded design representing the five Royal Palaces.

Keep the crown, keep the castle; a symbol for Windsor Castle, establishing its tourist potential.

Bath City Council, having been exposed to the possibilities of contemporary usage of traditional devices, decided that its coat of arms could perhaps be transmogrified into something that could sensibly be reproduced on its dustcarts without expensive and complicated heraldic intricacy. Hence the simplified block treatment of the crown/shield device which loses none of the royal tradition which so typifies the ethos of the city.

159

LOCATION IDENTITY

People, behaviour, images and environment are all tangible ingredients of identity. But geography is also important - the area of location is a powerful contributory factor to the perception of an organisation. This is often a question of *force majeure;* a high street chain obviously needs to be on the high street but nevertheless in the appropriate location. BHS, for example, has always endeavoured to be adjacent to Marks and Spencer, a mutually beneficial and synergistic location policy.

However, in order to establish a particular kind of credibility lawyers tend to congregate in Lincoln's Inn, financial services cluster round the stock exchange and art galleries fall over themselves in Cork Street. There is a suspicion that to move outside these hallowed areas is to somehow downgrade the offer. A solicitor in the Finchley Road or a gallery in Putney simply does not have the same *cachet* as 'better'-located colleagues - expectations are lower from those who are not party to the location club. Large high-profile organisations on the other hand can afford to break this rule - witness the mushrooming of head offices between Chiswick and Swindon, for example.

The cost implications are paradoxical; the small low-profile company will and often does pay dearly to locationally belong, while the multinationals will save fortunes by re-locating out of town. Wall Street and the City mean something specific in terms of the perception of those companies which operate from these areas. Docklands means something else: the pioneering spirit, as does Mayfair: the well-heeled periphery.

WH Smith's head office re-location from central London to Swindon in the early 1980s did nothing to dent its image. Although its original building was designed by Sir Hugh Casson, its current HQ was commissioned from Ahrends/Burton/Koralek - one of the most highly regarded architectural practices in the UK, despite their problems with their National Gallery extension proposals dubbed 'carbuncle' by Prince Charles.

PEOPLE POWER

The notion of a uniformed contract security guard who, incarcerated in a glass box, demands identification prior to issuing a plastic tag with an impossible clip device which is supposed to be attached to clothing in the manner of criminals being photographed for police records is not, in the interests of presenting an organisation in the best possible light, a happy one to be greeted with on entering a reception area. It is, however, a scenario often encountered when entering the premises of a large organisation - especially those attached to government or officialdom of any kind.

The apparent necessity for electronic tunes to be played into the telephone earpiece in order to disguise the inefficiency of the telephonist is a dire piece of subterfuge which does little to enhance a company's credibility and a secretary employed for the sole purpose of beating off individuals who wish to communicate with her boss is a dubious asset for a company who wishes to present an open friendly face to the world. These nightmares are by no means fantasy, and are encountered every day even within organisations which in other respects appear to be quite human and well organised. As discussed elsewhere, people are the company and if rigorous attention is not paid to their behaviour, manner and appearance the whole identity edifice can be undermined. Training programmes are now available for every eventuality, from teaching the chief executive to weather an inquisition on TV to appraising a secretary on how to answer the telephone correctly. A good receptionist is expensive - but then so is a lost client.

Reception areas need as a pre-requisite to be enviromentally agreeable - but so do the people behind the desk.

COLOUR

Red: roses, blood, aggression, Communist

Green: ecology, envy, slime, money

Blue: sky, distance, cold, fresh

Yellow: sun, hot, flower, coward

Black: death, night, fear, magic

White: snow, purity, blank, wedding

Red disc = Japan

Red + Green discs = stop/go

Red + Green vertical bars = Italy

A blue rose is a disturbing paradox

A red sky means evening

Colour is an emotive and potentially expressive tool in terms of visual identity and depends for its effect on two quite separate considerations: association with natural phenomena and association with received cultural references.

The GMB's new, softer identity is emphasised by the use of an orange/blue combination, replacing the previous confrontational black/red scheme. Apple Computers' multi-colour treatment implies range and versatility, while Harrods' particular shade of green, redolent of deep and expensive leather furniture, when combined with gold accurately hits the appropriate psychological target.

In the political arena, red is associated with left wing

attitudes; in the UK blue is associated with the right wing, while orange, the colour of compromise, represents the middle ground. Such is the emotive power of colour, albeit from a received culture, that boards of directors with a leaning towards the political right will often refuse to entertain the use of red for their corporate colour. If, however, it is used with blue, they will be inclined to accept it on the grounds of national pride.

Colour can surprise, shock, or delight; however, culture references such as 'pink for girls, blue for boys' or colours which simply illustrate a name - Black & Decker, Ward White - are unlikely to pass the global comprehension test. Colour can be used as an overall corporate statement or for divisional differentiation. It can signal character, attitude and function.

The colour of money - generally understood to be green - is the colour most often employed for financial institutions, and is, in fact, the corporate colour for De La Rue, who prints money. Shell's yellow/red combination is calculated to express warmth and welcome. ICI's dark blue exudes the responsible respectability expected of it.

The wild card is fashion and there are several highly respected organisations whose function is to predict the colours to which people will be most likely to respond in the future. The UK high street's background colour turned from brown in the seventies to grey in the eighties. Atlanta Airport for example is entirely a reflection of the eighties decade in which it was upgraded - grey and pink abounds. White or off-white is now appearing in the nineties, perhaps reflecting a new purity. In the world of clothes fashion, often a pointer to where colour preferences will surface in other areas, there is a strong movement towards the use of unbleached and undyed fabrics, possibly a result of our new-formed ecological responsibility. Off-white jeans may well translate to off-white visual identities.

Motor cars were black with red stripes in the late seventies, metallised pastel by the mid-eighties, perhaps matt ecological green in the nineties? These vagaries need to be accounted for in the context of corporate identity; the problem is one of longevity and appropriateness tempered with fashion awareness.

De La Rue's green symbol - the colour of money.

THE TOTAL IDENTITY

There have been a number of well documented major corporations who have successfully embraced the notion of total identity - AEG, Olivetti, IBM - but it is comparatively rare for medium or small organisations to effect such a comprehensive statement. Sufficient resources, both human and financial, are not generally voted for such an exercise unless operating on a global stage.

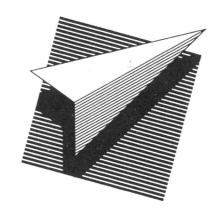

LONDON CITY
AIRPORT

London City Airport; a total identity. Practical environment (the LCA product), targeted ambience (the offer) graphic identity (exterior/interior manifestation).

As with BMW, the product *is* the identity. A specific target consumer group is identified; in this case the business traveller. Every aspect of his expectations needs to be not only expected but fulfilled. An integrated design approach to ambience, logistics, offer, and the visual expression of these elements in environmental and graphic terms is calculated to produce a seamless entity which is not only real but projected as such.

The synthesis between the intent and the perceived and experienced reality is something which can only be achieved by the designers' total involvement from the conception of the business idea to its eventual fruition. Signage echoes the corporate statement.

This is perhaps understandable, but the advantages which can accrue to a medium sized operation are proportionately the same as those for a multinational. In 1981 the UK construction company John Mowlem, following discussions with the London Docklands Development Corporation, decided to embark on a unique project - the creation of a businessman's airport within immediate reach of the City of London. It would offer a high-quality environment, speed of check-in, short journey times and, unusual for a British airport, excellent catering facilities.

As the 9,000 square metre £32 million development was to be unlike any other airport catering for a specific market, it was essential that the total offer should be accurately targeted in every respect; its identity would be created and communicated not simply by graphic devices, but by every facet of its environment, its staff and its service. Airport interiors are generally sterile and uninspiring, associated with long hours of unrelaxed waiting. In this case, the ambience was to be targeted to a specific market - the identity of the project being the product itself rather than any isolated graphic representation.

Airport retail strategy does not normally contribute either to the identity of the environment or to its aesthetic. In the case of London City, the business traveller would have little time to spend landside before checking in. He would however require newsagents, banking, car and hotel booking facilities and a flower stall to placate his wife on a possible late arrival. Despite the obvious disparity of the various offers, these concessions were designed to have a controlled appearance in harmony with the overall atmosphere of the terminal without diminishing the identities of the individual traders. It is probably unique that Hertz, for example, agreed to this strategy - a measure of its recognition of the value of an overall identity as opposed to a free-for-all.

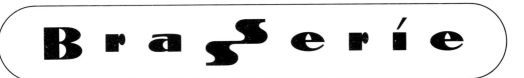

London City Airport's subsidiary identity for the main restaurant.

Catering within airport environments is rarely a stimulus to appetite; in the case of London City, the eating requirements of the business traveller were analysed and solutions found which would positively contribute to the overall proposition. The London City Brasserie with its own sub-identity was established, the atmosphere of which was calculated to reflect a more acceptable approach to airport catering. No fixed plastic seating and self-service queues.

Signage is crucial in terms of information and passenger movement, but in the context of total identity it can become a powerful and sympathetic visual statement. The approach in this instance bears little relationship to the insistent yellow/blue visual bombardment employed by most other travel environments. People accustomed to finding their way around airport terminals do not need the overstated, over-signed messages typical of the large international airports. The tone and colours of the directional signage programme echo the graphic corporate theme. The typeface was chosen to achieve a balance between function and aesthetics, and to represent the intended classic and contemporary values which characterise the overall approach. Commercial, as opposed to directional, signage is designed in such a way as to ensure that each concession outlet has an equal voice and does not conflict visually or detract from the intended ambience.

At the centre of the identity scheme is the symbol, depicting flight over the Square Mile; this device, however, is only a small part of the total identity concept, but one which, when detached from its environment, serves as a positive identification tag.

The graphic and environmental components of the London City identity were developed concurrently; not, as in many instances, at different times and in different places. This is not always logistically possible, but when it is, the end result can be a coherent and focused entity to which the customer, client, and the public at large can positively relate,

6 Aspects of Visual Identity

A corporate identity is the summation of a set of characteristics specific to a particular organisation. These characteristics can be altered or re-aligned by thoughtful management rather in the way that individuals, in the context of their immediate society, tend to suppress the more disagreeable aspects of their natures while enhancing those which they consider to be attractive.

The successful manipulation of emphasis in either case depends on an objective self knowledge allied to an understanding of exterior perceptions. A good tailor can exteriorise the personality of an individual - as a good designer can encapsulate and communicate the culture and ethos of a corporate body.

The designer speaks on two levels - intellectual and emotional, and it is this balance which, if correctly targeted, will elicit the appropriate response. Research and analysis can identify the problems, the business management consultant can correct them and the designer communicate the result with whatever individual talent and received culture he might possess.

The French Ministry of Culture (Le Ministère de la Culture) approached Peter Saville and Associates in conjunction with Sharon Ellis to develop a visual identity which would encapsulate its function while not cluttering promotional material produced by its 'client' organisations which would almost certainly contain other identity devices. The pure simplicity of the solution has a style and openness which is entirely appropriate to its function. The lateral thinking employed in arriving at such a device is a refreshing departure from the endless captioned pictograms now so much in evidence.

'Commercial Art' was a term eschewed by Eric Gill.

Gill wished to return to the values of classicism - the book beautiful, the purity of form, the aesthetic values associated with ancient Greece and Rome. Classic letter forms; originally created by the cut of the chisel on stone with the mechanistic thick downstrokes and thin upstrokes, the finishing of linear statements with what we now know as 'serifs', were to him sacrosanct, even though translated into the alien medium of print.

His, and like-minded others' dedication to these notions succeeded in projecting WH Smith in its formative years as being a responsible, literate, credible and relevant organisation. This was later to be somewhat eroded by neglect but Gill's design influence was undoubtedly a major factor in the growth of the company in the earlier part of this century.

FASHION AND DURABILITY

The way in which the visual elements of an identity come together as a style statement depends to a large extent on the influences of fashion - the accepted visual vernacular of the time.

172

WH Smith's first coherent visual identity emerged in 1903 with Eric Gill's elegant 'book beautiful' lettering supported, in 1905, by an egg-shaped monogrammatic symbol designed by RP Gossop and later by a newsboy device designed by Septimus Scott.
All these elements were co-ordinated by what we would now call a design manager - Frank Bayliss - into a visual statement which exactly echoed the prevalent stylistic aspirations of the early twentieth century; refined roman typography and literal pen rendered illustrations.

The great and perhaps unfortunately enduring typeface of the 1960s: Helvetica. No serifs, no nonsense, no character, but 'my God you can read it'. A calculated rationalisation of letter forms. Gill's retention of the serif, the thick/thin character of type created by chisel and quill pen was abandoned on the altar of rationalisation. But where is the Soul? A whole design vernacular sprang up around this Swiss product of ordered cleanliness in the 1960s. Motorway signage, largely based on the principles established by Helvetica, benefited from high legibility factors created by the balance of the spaces within the letter forms and the structure of the letters themselves.

Visual identity programmes abounded based on the ordered coolness of the face; the Bath Festival symbol is such a product - totally unsuited in character to the event it represented, but nevertheless well within the given visual language of the time. The Brighton Festival symbol, although in a similar vernacular, works somewhat better due to less uncompromising form.

In the late 1950s and early 1960s, Swiss typography exerted a powerful influence on European corporate identity design. It could be said that the uncompromising typefaces designed at the time, such as Helvetica and Univers, and their strict geometric arrangement were a natural extension of the Swiss character. Symbols became a mirror of this visual culture, with their even-thickness linear geometry.

At about the same time in the United States the antithesis of this approach, the West Coast flower power graphics of Peter Max, et al, was becoming a major influence on identity design. Free form, sometimes even psychedelic schemes emerged representing a transatlantic cultural counterpoint.

By the 1970s, European designers were tending to react against the Swiss austerity, and a freer, more illustrative approach to identity was evident. Fletcher/Forbes/Gill was one of the first design

174

consultancies in the UK to break away from what they considered to be the limiting conventions of the Swiss and were as a consequence a major influence in the development of identity design during the period.

Fine art influences were also starting to appear; Bridget Riley's Op Art and the American Pop Movement (itself a pastiche of commercial design) surfaced from time to time in identity programmes.

The 1980s will doubtless be remembered for the influence of Matisse - Wolff Olins' Prudential being the prime example. In a sense, this was the result of a desire to continue Fletcher/Forbes/Gill's crusade to free up the genre - to put a more human and accessible face on companies and corporations. Future influences are difficult to predict, but the communications explosion of the 1980s and its knock- on effect of the development of global commerce will undoubtedly require designers to develop a more universal visual language.

Fletcher/Forbes/Gill (now Pentagram)'s proposal for the visual exteriorisation of the National Theatre, designed in the early 1970s but never adopted, symbolises the breakaway from the influence of Swiss austerity.

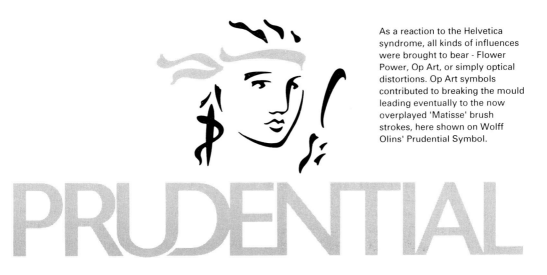

As a reaction to the Helvetica syndrome, all kinds of influences were brought to bear - Flower Power, Op Art, or simply optical distortions. Op Art symbols contributed to breaking the mould leading eventually to the now overplayed 'Matisse' brush strokes, here shown on Wolff Olins' Prudential Symbol.

The CEGB three wired 'e' lasted as long as the organisation itself, while the "Concept for Men" logotype, was only ever intended to make a style statement for a single season. Durability is not necessarily a virtue, especially in the fashion world.

It is of course reasonable for an organisation to wish to eschew any visual influence which might wane in the public consciousness. Longevity is in most instances a virtue, given the sometimes serious cost of change. In 1960 the Central Electricity Generating Board had no premonition of its eventual demise, and therefore understandably required its new identity to have lasting qualities. The three wired 'e' was deliberately designed with maximum simplicity - no references or concessions being made to previous or contemporary visual vernaculars.

On the other hand, organisations overtly concerned with fashion would not be best served by such an approach. Chelsea Girl, a chain of fashion shops aimed at the youth culture, deliberately change its visual identity every two years. The dots and squiggles designed in 1986 belong strictly to that year and were designed to do so. They do however most certainly appear extremely dated today.

However potentially permanent a set of visual components may appear to be, it is in the long term inevitable that they will become irrelevant. Heraldry is only marginal today, it being little understood and representing as it does a single notion - establishment. Swiss geometry has already passed out of the designer's vocabulary, as has psychedelia and pop art. Visual vernaculars are sometimes revived, as with Bauhaus typography or Matisse's brush strokes, but these pastiche statements are generally short-lived being the product of desperation to find a different (but not necessarily original) visual solution.

CULTURAL INFLUENCE

Influences on the style and visual form of a corporate identity are not solely confined to fashionable mores. The overall cultural climate of any given society will largely determine the approach. In terms of visual literacy television, for example, has transformed those societies in which it operates, where sophisticated imagery is readily understood and appreciated. Likewise the wit and humour of the best advertising has conditioned its recipients to respond to subtle or oblique visual statements.

The Japanese are influenced by the elegance of their calligraphy, the Americans by their tradition of hard sell marketing, the British by their pragmatism.

The quality of national educational systems will determine the level of intellectual content which can be inculcated into an identity solution. There is however always a danger of overestimating society's knowledge and intelligence; the designer had obviously been aware of Prudential's Prudence, but it is less certain that the general public understands the reference without being told. Conversely, an underestimation can simply lead to condescension - an irritating trait, if perceived.

A simple but explicit logotype implying function.

The most powerful influence on the form and content of a visual identity can be the client - the 'my wife/husband likes blue' syndrome is by no means unusual and can become a major source of contention when the consultant intends employing green for the excellent reason that the company involved concerns itself with forestry. On the other hand, it is the client's (if the his wife's/husband's) culture which is to be reflected, and this input is crucial.

EXTERNAL FACTORS

External influences outside the control of an organisation can force a change of direction and therefore identity. The London Zoo, for decades dedicated to the whims of research scientists at the expense of paying customers, found itself on the edge of bankruptcy (and will probably continue to do so). It being a national institution, the government shelled out a million pounds to save it - but that in itself cannot be sufficient. Money can repair crumbling walls and stave off starvation of the animals, but it cannot by itself alter a culture.

Sir Solly Zuckerman, who had dedicated his career to highly respected and world acclaimed achievements in zoology retired, opening the way to a radical change of direction for the zoo to become self supporting, to embrace the notion of commercialism.

Just at the moment when the corner was about to be turned with a new marketing based venture with all that that implies, the Greens decreed that urban based zoos are against the best interests of world ecology - in a word, cruel. In a relatively short space of time, the culture of the organisation had been forcibly changed from high academic research to marketing based entertainment: something which is at best considered suspect by an increasingly vociferous pressure group. From establishment to entrepreneurism to defensiveness - different forced cultures which need to be expressed in different visible terms. Adroit footwork at management level and a flexible approach to identity design are pre-requisites for survival in the face of changing circumstances not always subject to internal control.

Although external influences control and often confuse management decisions, internal strife can be even more difficult to deal with in identity terms. How to express a coherent offer if it is in itself subject to opposing and diffuse attitudes? The creation of the UK Social Democratic Party (SDP) in 1984 was the result of market forces - the filling of a political vacuum perceived by a group of disaffected leading politicians from various persuasions. Ill-prepared in terms of a coherent and comprehensible policy, curiously incompatible in terms of the relationships between the main personalities involved and relying on a negative vote factor (disaffection) is no recipe for the creation of a believable identity.

Design consultancies were indeed consulted, but there is little that even the most sophisticated process could have achieved in projecting a believable concept given the circumstances. The scenario gets worse: the party splits; various members join another minority party, a long-established and well respected group of politically mature people who were the inheritors of a credible (but numerically much diminished) grouping of marginal interests.

David Owen, the remaining founder-member of the SDP, a man of many and admirable qualities, decides to stick it out and for better or worse retain the identity of the organisation in all its manifestations and maintain the individuality of the idea as it first existed. Meanwhile, the long-established Liberal Party, which the defectors joined, was thrown into a serious identity crisis. The old guard, the new guard, and now defectors from an even newer guard had somehow to be incorporated into a coherent whole; nomenclature became the subject of seemingly endless and acrimonious debate.

The Liberal Democrats finally decided on a name - and a symbol, designed by Fitch & Co.

The Liberal Democrats, the Democratic Liberals, the Social Democrats, the Social Democratic Liberals, the Liberal Democratic Party, the Democratic Liberal Party and so on. The emotive question of identity raged for a considerable and unproductive period, during which time the fortunes of the party diminished in direct proportion to its indecision.

No discernible intellectual, political or visual hook emerged for either the new political concept or the supposedly rejuvenated established party, leaving its competitors where they were - unassailable. It was only when the name, and its visual expression, were finally decided upon that its fortunes turned.

Political groupings, as with commercial enterprises, will not survive without clearly defined objectives and cultural attitudes. Visual manifestations of non-events is a contradiction in terms and it is not surprising that the sorry chain of political events surrounding the proposed resurgence of British radical politics was for a time virtually stillborn. The emergence of a clear statement of intent in both intellectual and visual terms saved the day.

MARKET FORCES

Large and long-established commercial organisations are subject to the same problems which confront the first officer of a mega-oil tanker. Both are unwieldy and slow to take avoiding action. By the nature of things, ascendency balances decline in the market-place. Some win, some lose; new concepts struggle upwards while old ones, unless they are prepared to be flexible and invent some steering mechanisms to change direction towards relevancy, will decline.

In identity terms the decline or survival of religions is

CONSERVATIVE

Labour

a useful comparison to commercial corporations.
In the West, Roman Catholicism has for the moment
a more effective and cogent power base than
Anglicanism; not because it is necessarily any more
attractive as a culture/faith but because it is more
focused in its ritual and symbolism. Its identity is
effectively controlled and policed and its adherents
understand exactly what it has to offer. In predominantly
Catholic societies, people still by and large attend
church services, eat fish on Fridays and eschew
divorce and mechanical contraception.

In the Anglican faith, there is a certain desperation about
the way in which they strive to be relevant - trendy
clergy in grey silk shirts and turn down collars - the
drive for the ordination of women - jazz in the crypt.
These outward manifestations of sociological relevancy
have simply not worked in terms of recruitment because
the outward trappings do not reflect any substantive or
immutable direction - a paradox which many companies
have found to be disastrous.

Meanwhile and elsewhere, Islam has recently and
probably momentarily been in the ascendancy, linked
as it is with revolutionary politics and the emotive
power of images of a dead Ayatollah being paraded as
an ultimate icon.

As with large commercial organisations, all this will
change. External influences and pressures - market
forces - dictate the way in which cultures evolve and

182

project themselves. Islam will decline in influence as the politicians, having exploited the short-term emotive advantage, become more relevant in their own right. The images, slogans and all the aggressive symbolism will need to devolve and be replaced at the same pace. Problems occur, as in Iraq, when devolution is out of step.

Roman Catholicism will bow to the pressure of such fundamental world pressures as over population and social conditions in underdeveloped countries and modify its dogmas. Its rich ornate symbolism will also need to change to reflect its new relevance to ordinary people.

The Anglicans will either decline further into an anachronistic irrelevance or be forced to reassert a coherent doctrine in order to survive. If there is to be a renaissance, this will need to be powerfully communicated by a rejuvenated and vibrant identity programme geared to vie with other more commercially oriented leisure activities such as TV, theatre and film.

Given the 'Global village' notion, fuelled by the 1980s technological explosion in the communications field, cultural flexibility is now an essential part of any organisation's development, and corporate identity must synchronise with the constant pragmatic shifts in attitude and direction which will need to be taken in the interests of survival.

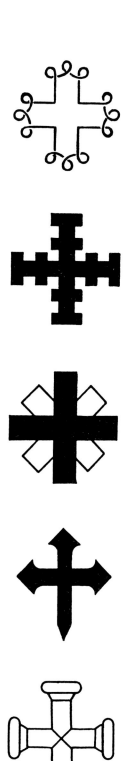

PROBLEMS

It would be naive to suppose that so long as all the ground rules are adhered to, a successful identity programme will inevitably emerge. Personalities may clash, resulting in diminishing commitment; internal politics can wreck the best planned programme; visual solutions can be diluted by committee.

Crosfield Electronics, formally a subsidiary of De La Rue, is a hi-tech company engaged in the highly competitive field of electronic imaging and transmission with world-wide interests. In 1986 it was decided to create a new visual identity which would reflect its pre-eminence in its field.

Research was undertaken; first class air trips to New York, extensive visits to US based clients in the comfort of a chauffeur driven stretch limo, interviews in its New Jersey office (expensive top management time), visits to its UK based R&D centres and so on. A report was duly delivered and agreed; the brief was clear. Two visual schemes were developed in parallel within the confines of the consultancy and presented to the board. Indecision resulted in neither being accepted or developed; instead a feeble compromise was stitched together 'in house'.

The moral of the tale is that the development of a corporate identity should be a joint effort - the consultancy and the client working closely together from initial sketch stage through to the final presentation. There should be no surprises, no doubts; choice should be eliminated at the early stages in order to avoid expensive mistakes. The company has since been sold to a competitor who will doubtless reassess the situation yet again.

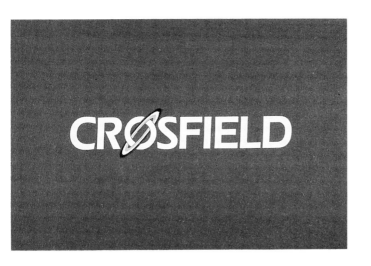

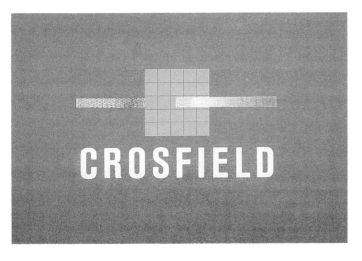

Two alternative proposals for the visual identity of an international company concerned with hi-tech imaging for the printing industry. One aspect of its systems is the transmission by satellite of fully scanned colour photographs. In the event, neither of these proposals was accepted, the client preferring to produce his own solution. Life is full of disappointments.

National Westminster Bank

In 1987 the National Westminster Bank, along with most of their competitors, decided to re-orient its High Street image towards a more retail based environment; open banking, product based offers, accessability. The new statement was to be both graphic and environmental; a total package involving everything from space planning to signage, from carpets to cheque books, from open non-fortress tills to lighting.

The graphic identity, designed in the 1960s, was (and at the time of writing still is) built around a somewhat dour and aggressive black and white fragmented triangle, apparently denoting the coming together of the three banks from which NatWest was formed. Although there was no suggestion that this device should be abandoned, it was evident that some adaptation was essential in order to more accurately reflect the new less remote and more human face of contemporary banking. Thus, the graphic and environmental considerations were developed simultaneously, they being the constituent parts of the total visual identity.

The symbol was lightened, three-dimensionalised and given some 'movement' by introducing a comb effect on the three angled planes and, for signage, a three colour spectrum was applied to the three components. Halfway through the development stage, it was decided that the cost of these adjustments in terms of their application across the board was unacceptable. The result: an environmental identity divested of any

186

corporate presence other than a somewhat contradictory set of 1960s graphic components. An understandable situation created by force of circumstances, but one which is less than ideal.

Until the full implications and mechanics of corporate identity as a major business resource are fully understood by both client and consultancy alike, these kinds of problems will doubtless persist.

Aspects of a repositioning exercise for the National Westminster Bank, The brief was to humanise what was perceived as a somewhat forbidding and authoritarian institution. In corporate identity terms, environment and graphic presentation were considered in tandem. Unfortunately, only a few basic concepts have been adopted for the interior environment, while the graphic renovations have been shelved.

A proposal for the updating of a well-known device originated in the 1960s. By 'combing' parts of the elements, a lighter, more three-dimensional and more contemporary statement is achieved. Unfortunately never realised.

TIMING

Early in 1989, Stephen Barker who was chief executive of a large and successful company decided to go out on his own. With help from the financial institutions, he acquired an ailing company in the apparently unpromising field of manufacture and distribution of down-market hosiery, sold mainly through grocery chains. Other synergistic companies were acquired along the way; within less than a year, the holding company was rated third in the City's share price increase index in a period of quasi-depression; a remarkable achievement.

The identity problem however was, under understandable management time pressure, relegated to the back burner, even though it had been seriously considered from the start. The name of the original acquired company, Glamar, was suited to its core product but less than convincing for a major force in the City.

An identity strategy was therefore devised whereby Glamar would be retained as an exclusive brand name for the 'grocery chain' hosiery products, a new name and authoritative visual identity devised for the holding company and floating decisions made as to how to present the new companies and their products as they became acquired, taking into account their market synergy with the existing structure at any given time.

188

All trading companies however would be endorsed by the new holding company name in order, through a strata of markets, to establish its credibility as a serious contender in the City. A reasoned and sensible strategy.

In the event, the success of the holding company overtook itself in identity terms. To change its image to the City after a year of high profile success is a daunting task not to be undertaken by the faint hearted. A decision was, however, finally taken to re-name the holding company 'Hartstone', a name derived from the directors' personal associations, but given the pressure which had accrued it was a decision inevitably taken in some haste. Only time will tell whether the 'better late than never' approach will prove to have been correct, but it is clear that decisions on identity become more difficult in direct proportion to their deferment.

ENDORSEMENT

The London Zoo, as mentioned earlier, has experienced a series of changes to its essential culture and *raison d'être*, culminating in a market oriented attempt, against various odds, to communicate an 'entertainment for the family' offer. The graphic imagery, however, serves only to illustrate the transition - a compromise between the *ancien régime* of institutional academia and the new-found, pragmatic necessity to entertain. A banal and probably

London and Whipsnade Zoos endorsed by 'common ownership' coat of arms; curious, though, that they choose to differentiate by the use of different typefaces.

unauthorised coat of arms inexplicably surmounts a contemporary and well-executed rendering of the essential offer. Its subsidiary operation - the Whipsnade 'Wild Animal Park' - although embracing the London Zoo's basic visual elements (including the heraldic device) perversely chooses to employ a different typestyle.

The balance between corporate membership and corporate ownership is often delicate, even in real terms, but to visually exteriorise this confusion is both unnecessary and impolitic. Either Whipsnade is the same offer as London Zoo or it is not.
In marketing as in visual terms, this requires focused clarification in order to avoid consumer disillusionment or disappointment.

Endorsement is a complicated matter, often exacerbated by corporate pride. To be seen to own everything in sight is an egotempt not easily resisted. In the same way that a retail chain targeted towards the teenage market should not be perceived as owned by an Establishment organisation, so it should not be evident that an international bank is run by an advertising agency. It would have been interesting to see how Saatchi planned to project Midland Bank's identity if its proposed takeover had succeeded.

Anomalies abound. Why is a construction company owned by Taylor Woodrow called Myton with the

Taylor Woodrow symbol as an endorsement? Staying with the construction industry, why should a shipping company (P&O) be seen to endorse the accurately tailored Bovis identity? Why should the Rover Group choose to dissipate its valuable MG marque by applying it to slow, cheap cars?

Strange and confusing images are presented to the world at large by the endorsement system. Although palpably the result of the machinations of finance, takeovers and mergers, relationships between owners and operators are fogged by their presentation. Endorsement should be used positively, communicating the advantages of connection, emphasising the strength of the whole being stronger and more credible than the individual parts. Political expediency is irrelevant in marketing terms; the customer is king; his perception is paramount.

Endorsement can, if handled correctly, be a positive and constructive marketing device. The royal coat of arms lends a certain credibility to selected goods and services (although whether the Queen actually consumes the marmalade or chocolates so endorsed is an intriguing question). Large and stable institutions such as Trafalgar House lend weight and financial muscle to their operating companies (although Hanson does not take this route) and there is no doubt that Cadbury's endorsement sells chocolate cream cakes, even if they are manufactured by someone else.

Corporate endorsement is not always readily understood by the consumer or end-user. Why, for example, does Bovis, a building contractor, need acknowledge the parenthood of a shipping company?

There are usually good reasons for taking these identity routes; addressing different markets, promoting the diversity and scale of a holding company, or simply signalling credibility are all valid reasons for endorsement. However, if not carefully handled in terms of visual relationships, the non-cognoscenti can be faced with bewildering messages.

Competing petrol companies adopting different visual stances.

Shell: a straightforward depiction of the name which through massive and carefully orchestrated exposure has succeeded in becoming visually synonymous with the product.

COMPARISONS

Individual companies operating within an increasing number of industries are now, through rationalisation, market forces or legal regulation, in a position where their products or services do not differ in any discernible way from those of their competitors. As noted elsewhere in this book, it is their personality which can set them apart - in marketing terms, it is their visual identity which expresses this difference in culture and can signal their uniqueness and desirability to the consumer. The petrol market is one such; all the players offering an identical product to a consumer who would rather not have to be involved - in short, a distress purchase with no product choice. To fill the car is a major irritation. There is no service, the product smells disagreeable and tends to slop on to clothing, it is expensive and seems not to go very far. The whole experience is a necessary but unwelcome interruption to an otherwise bearable existence. Petrol companies have therefore invested more than most in competitive and compelling visual identities.

Shell's corporate identity was born in 1901 when the founder named his company in reverence to the fact that his dad collected shells - an outrageously unacceptable notion in today's climate of market research and analysis. However, with expert design management over the years, the visual identity has evolved from being centred around a somewhat scratchy drawing of a mussel to a sophisticated

192

graphic rendering of a coquille St Jacques by
Raymond Loewy dating from 1971.

The fact that the visual device is an illustration of the
name (at least in English-speaking environments) adds
visual strength and focus, typography being an almost
unnecessary visual adjunct. Through massive but well
orchestrated exposure throughout the world, it could
be claimed that this is also true in foreign language
countries - coquillage or concha are not words which
spring readily to mind on encountering the symbol in
France or Spain-nevertheless the power of the image
ensures its comprehension.

Interestingly, Shell claims that if its visual identity
were to be abandoned, extra expenditure on
advertising would run into millions of pounds a year
in order to maintain its market share. However, the
weakness of the visual identity is that it says nothing
about the character of the products of Shell, nor
about its customers - it speaks not on any emotional
level. If the symbol as it is now had never been
associated with a petrol company, it would not be out
of place outside the Folies Bergères, resembling as it
does, without preconceived associations, a lady's fan.

It is perhaps because of this that certain competitors
have decided to take a different route - BP's
penetration of the green culture or Q8's visual/verbal
pun which is calculated to involve customers on a
more human level. Although their visual identity has

BP monogram: part of a
complicated promotional
campaign calculated to conjure
up feelings of 'all good things
British'.

193

been much misunderstood, with wild claims in the media of the 'million pound symbol', the reality is that the notion of repositioning the company involved a complex set of interrelated factors - an advertising campaign establishing its Britishness and responsibility towards the environment, the re-design and construction of its filling stations nationwide and the complicated process of re-organising all printed matter.

Mobil has a chequered corporate identity history, culminating in a confused melange of flying horses and a somewhat soulless 1960s logotype. In the late nineteenth century, the company started life as the Vacuum Oil Company, its visual identity being supported by wacky illustrations in the later style of Heath Robinson. The product, however, was named Mobil Oil, both names being given equal visual emphasis.

In 1904 the company decided that it needed some visual device to signal its products, and a trademarks agent working for Vacuum at the time hit upon a notion that out-punned even Q8 - Gargoyle.
The result of this flash of insight was that the products were labelled Gargoyle Vacuum Mobil Oil, capped with a dragon-like creature poised to topple from its perch. This device was inexplicably joined in 1947 by a flying red horse.

The horse eventually won the unequal struggle, vanquishing the gargoyle and thus becoming the main

Mobil

Mobil: a relatively new logotype curiously married to the much older device of the flying horse. This company has passed through a number of metamorphoses during its history from being originally the Vacuum Oil Co through to the excruciating pun of Gargoyle.

company symbol - 'the spirit of flying horsepower'. In 1955, the holding company sensibly changed its name to Mobil Oil Company and in 1966 the visual namestyle was developed into the current predominantly blue Helvetica typeface with the red 'O'.

Curiously, the flying horse was retained, and continues to hover over filling stations to this day. Over the years, the company has endeavoured to appear relevant, even at one point to the extent of dressing its petrol pump attendants in miniskirts and hotpants, but the end result lacks the conviction of Shell or the humanity and national identity of BP.

Esso appears dated, Texaco aggressive, Exxon bland and Elf overbearing. All these competitive companies elicit different emotional responses through their nomenclature and visual identities, some for the better, some for the worse. In a crowded single marketplace, identity is all important.

BRANDING AND IDENTITY

The dividing line between an 'identity' and a 'brand' is often a grey area and one which, if misunderstood or misapplied, can lead to considerable confusion. Marlboro cigarettes (brand) are manufactured by Philip Morris Products Inc (an identity, but also another brand). Cadbury's chocolate (brand) is manufactured by Cadbury/Schweppes (an identity, but also two brands). Unilever on the other hand

196

does not lend its name to any of its brands, while BMW unequivocally does.

The 'own brand' syndrome employed by most large store chains is no more clear cut. 'St Michael' is employed as a brand by Marks and Spencer while Tesco uses its own name for its own products. There are no rules; pragmatism reigns. However, the purpose and function of brands in relation to identity has to be clearly understood in each individual instance.

Anchor Foods, for example, wanted to develop its name as a brand to be applied across other dairy products to be developed, thus diversifying and expanding its product range due to pressure from EC quotas restricting the import of New Zealand butter. The brief required only an imperceptible change to the existing butter pack while at the same establishing a useable brand image doubling as a corporate identity device for future development and expansion. A tallish order accomplished by the careful manipulation of the original graphic devices into a central visually coherent statement.

The new corporate identity developed from a brand has been used across the company on all its facets including buildings, vehicle livery and stationery. The pack was successfully redesigned without losing any existing customer loyalty but incorporated key changes in the presentation of information. Anchor Foods have successfully applied its new

Before and after. An unusual problem of creating a visual identity from a well-known pack design without the consumer being overtly aware of change. The company decided to diversify its product range and flag its corporate presence on vehicles, buildings, new product packs, etc. No visual elements on the existing pack were suitable for this exercise; an amalgam of the most recognisable devices was therefore created for use on all visible facets of the company's activities.

This pragmatic approach to visual identity, while not perhaps being the most innovative, has the inescapable logic of exploiting existing recognition factors.

identity to an extensive range of dairy products gaining a rapid market share increase.

Brand Value

In 1988, Grand Metropolitan announced that it would henceforth include the value of its recently acquired brands in its balance sheet. Including Smirnoff, the world's second best selling vodka, the total brands' value was pegged at what at the time seemed to be a staggering £500 million. Rank Hovis McDougall and Cadbury Schweppes followed suit by valuing their brands at £678 million and £307 million respectively. Guinness, United Biscuits and Reckitt & Coleman have all inflated their balance sheets by this means.

The ploy enables companies to raise City finance for acquisitions and expansion without referral to shareholders and although the accountancy profession views the inclusion of intangible assets in balance sheets with some suspicion and wishes to impose an amortisation period on their value, the City is prepared to swallow the notion, thereby endorsing the power of strong branding.

It is not only in the consumer goods sector that financial value can be related to branding. If for example a financial services holding company wishes to divest itself of an operating wing it will be a more desirable proposition if it is correctly and strongly branded.

A brand identity is more than a marketing device and more than the expression of a product or service; it has a tangible realisable value, often far in excess of the cost of its introduction.

Different market levels targeted by the same company.
A conceptual balance whereby the endorsement of the product originator needs to be equal credibility across a market range represented by different visual treatments.

Cult Identity

Mickey Mouse *is* the Disney Organisation. Grown men will sport a Mickey Mouse T-shirt or watch, while they might have second thoughts about depicting Care Bears or My Little Pony on their beachwear. The reasons for this phenomenon are complex, probably unplanned in the early stages of development, and often highly profitable.

The Pop Art movement of the 1960s opened the door to the acceptance of certain hitherto culturally unacceptable images as cult icons. The use of a certain level of tackiness and deliberately low-brow subject matter (but not too low) combined with careful contextual manipulation created a climate where Mickey, Brillo pads and vodka were OK while Reagan, military insignia and egg flip were not.

In the 1980s, certain fairly innocuous products or services emerged as representing the smart or 'yuppy' sector of society thereby creating and sometimes sustaining a market for themselves. A yellow plastic ashtray incorporating the Ricard logo became an essential part of any interior worth its social relevance. Pastis is not a product much favoured in British drawing rooms, but sales have nevertheless increased. A whole new dimension to the consumption of water was created by the combination of pastiche graphics, bottle shape and brilliant (if somewhat esoteric) advertising by Perrier. Furthermore, Perrier managed to survive a potentially disastrous obligatory, if temporary, withdrawal of its product from the marketplace due to contamination; companies with a less forceful image would have drowned. The Gitanes and Gauloises cigarette packets, designed in the early part of this century, must surely be the primary reason for their purchase, at least by Anglo-Saxons.

Porsche jackets, Dunhill scarves, and Jaguar sports bags are all instances where visual identities which represent 'lifestyle' in their primary product have been

Cult identities, all of which carry a heavy aura of nostalgia, but are none the worse for that.

The product as identity. Badges and labels are unnecessary for certain Joseph products which in themselves proclaim their origins. Joseph jumpers are known by all who need to know. BMW owners, however, often order their vehicles to be bereft of insignia.

profitably transferred to largely unrelated offers. There are obviously dangers in this transference of identity, and the assumption that a cult image can miraculously and automatically transform the desirability of an unrelated object should be taken with due consideration. Mickey perfectly signals time on an inexpensive watch, but would sit uncomfortably on a bottle of mineral water (mineral water, unlike time, is taken too seriously). Likewise, Perrier should not lend its name to cigarettes.

The original creation of a cult identity capable of eclectic application is an unlikely achievement. It is the core activity which it represents which, through exposure and acceptance, will create the base on which such a marketing strategy can be built.

Shades of Identity
A centralised and immutable visual identity scheme can, if not intelligently orchestrated, create a stranglehold on marketing efforts if different target audiences are involved. The design manual is a dangerous document if its rigidity does not allow for flexibility in the way in which visual elements can be manipulated. Professional bodies in particular have a need to communicate with a broad strata of targets - the Law Society speaks to its members, but also to the general public. Accountancy bodies target business, but at the same time need to recruit students. The same tone of voice employed for these different markets would almost certainly be inappropriate for some others.

202

Some pivotal visual components need to be retained in different applications in order to maintain the central identity - the use of symbols and logotypes as linch pins becomes crucial in these circumstances - but design attitudes need the freedom to be appropriate to the audience rather than the design manual if the required response is to be generated. A twenty-year-old student is unlikely to respond positively to a brochure designed to reach the senior fellows of the accountancy profession, just as captains of industry might feel reluctant to reach page two of a student publication.

If the visual environment in which the identity components exist creates the appropriate tone of voice, then the components themselves need to be designed in such a way as to be appropriate to a variety of treatments. Coats of arms, for example, patently do not fall into this category: too rigid an attitude to colour and supporting type styles might well be inhibiting factors and publication format restrictions, though often imposed in the interests of uniformity, can be inappropriate in marketing terms.

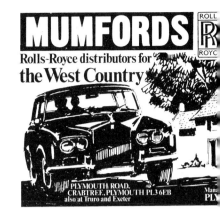

Elitism in extremis, where resentment often results in mascots being torn from bonnets, windows smashed and disfiguring grooves being carved along the length of the car. Image can be an expensive attribute, if only in repair costs.

Targeting

There used, in a real sense, to be social classes. Until the late 1930s there was the aristocracy, the upper-middle class, the middle class, the lower-middle class, and the working class; a simple but somewhat disagreeable system of classification.

Now we have a complicated but perhaps more socially acceptable hierarchy of socioeconomic designations, invented by advertising agencies, entirely based on income: A1 (no longer standing for 'aristocracy') A, B1, B2, C1, C2, D. These are the supposed groupings which need to be addressed in terms of marketing or corporate projection.

But who buys insurance, hamburgers, travel or T-shirts? Most people from every socioeconomic strata. On the other hand who buys private jets, Rolls Royce cars, Beluga caviar or 1926 port? The very affluent few or, more realistically, corporations wishing to reward their prime movers or clients in a manner befitting their status or their retention value. The top end, so to speak, is easier to target because it is a small sector of the market and therefore easier to define. From B to D however is amorphous, to say the least, and many goods and services need to address the entire spectrum for their basic offer. For this reason, organisations wishing to target a specific sector of their market will often need to speak with different tones of voice. Airlines for example have developed sub-identities or 'brands' in order to target the lucrative first- or business-class passenger. British Rail has followed suit by creating its 'Intercity' identity, while manufacturing companies position their products by means of a complicated hierarchy of names which imply status - General Motors' Carlton at the top end, Viva at the bottom.

INTERCITY

Sub-targeting to specific sectors of extremely large overall markets. Elitism is an inevitable ingredient of this approach, with hints of privilege and 'them and us'. However, if this were to be overplayed, the risk of resentment damaging the rest of the business could become a reality.

The alternative approach is to create a strong central identity covering all products or services which implies a consistent and expected level of quality across the board. BMW's products are only differentiated by numbers - 320, 520, 730, etc. Often, customers will request that even these designations are removed prior to delivery, thereby reinforcing the notion of the appeal of a single identity for a range of products.

Some people prefer to order their status symbols bereft of insignia.

If this approach is adopted, quality control needs to be extremely exacting if credibility is to be maintained. McDonalds, Olivetti and Marks and Spencer/ St Michael are all examples of the success of a single identity backed up by consistent and specific quality. The financial services sector on the other hand is more problematic; due to deregulations of various kinds a welter of parallel 'products' are now available from a variety of sources - banks, building societies, mortgage companies - and sub-branding systems need to be introduced in order to explain and differentiate the various offers. The danger is that the preminence of brands can dilute the corporate reputation - a balancing act which demands sensitive and intelligent handling.

INDIGENOUS OR IMPOSED IDENTITY

There are instances when the identity of a company is the product - no badges, corporate colours or typographic fine tuning is necessary to support the image if what is produced is sufficiently special or unique. A Rolls Royce car has no need of a flying lady perched on its bonnet - in any case banned in some countries for safety reasons - in order to project its message or market position.

A Chanel suit communicates a timeless and unmistakable 'brand' without having to read the label. Bang and Olufson hi-fi equipment, Laura Ashley dresses and Joseph jumpers all have unmistakable origins. On the other hand, the product can be the brand; a Lacoste T-shirt only has value if a small green crocodile is outwardly displayed; unexceptional sunglasses are sold for exorbitant prices due to a discreet endorsement by Porsche; sticks of inedible and dentally disastrous solidified pink sugar are sold to seaside visitors because some ingenious Victorian invented a method whereby the name of the resort could be incorporated longitudinally into the product.

A carefully exteriorised identity, whether indigenous or imposed, remains in all cases the purchase trigger. The power of visual identity cannot be overestimated; Brighton rock would not exist, Lacoste would not sell its T-shirts and Chanel suits would be shunned as being old-fashioned if it were not for the prestige attached to their perceived origins and image.

IMAGING

It is not only organisations or company policies which are made tangible by visual identity; events, ideas, environments even emotions, are all capable of being visually expressed. The Olympic Games have become a favourite game of the design profession, torturing the original interlinked circles into a series of national identities. The statutory government health warning on cigarette advertising has become as much a part of the image as the product itself, and has therefore ceased to engender fear. Conversely, a skull and crossbones printed on a bottle label is most definitely a deterrent to consuming its contents.

An emotive deterrent.

Every country has its own street, road and motorway identity created by the stylistic treatment of its particular signage systems. Football teams and their supporters identify themselves one with the other in no uncertain manner, as do old Etonians, pop groups and country squires. Theme parks, shopping centres, airports, cities, films, TV programmes, festivals, concerts; all have specific identities which can be expressed in an appropriate way, signalling not only function but individuality.

The identity of an idea - an ideogram - is not confined to Chinese calligraphy; a lavatory is identified by a silhouette of a man or woman - a complicated cultural notion which springs from our curious social requirement that the sexes should be segregated while performing their bodily functions.

Lavatory signs are understood only because of our cultural attitudes to sex segregation in this situation. An interesting aspect of symbolism which relies on oblique rather than direct communication. Perhaps in any event our social sensibilities would prohibit the use of a more direct approach.

Without this quirk, the symbols would mean nothing other than what they on the surface represent - a man or woman standing around doing nothing.

The idea of Communism is expressed by a star, but then so are Judaism and American generals. A star however is an illusion, the product of light reflected and refracted from a spherical planet. Stars are ascendant, emotional, beautiful. It is no accident that the word has been coined to describe famous film actors.

FAMILIARITY

We have come to accept that a red disc bisected by a white horizontal bar means 'no entry for vehicular traffic' although there is absolutely no logic in this visual statement. Continuing with traffic language, a symbol enclosed in a circle signals that the depicted object is forbidden - a curious and misguided notion, to say the least, especially when a different visual convention is used for 'no right turn' (ie: the turn is crossed out). An interesting quote from The Highway Code: 'These signs are mostly circular and those with red circles are mostly prohibitive'. Mostly?

The learning curve necessary to correctly interpret these signs is entirely cerebral and depends on familiarisation, as no visual logic exists. The same phenomenon can be observed in many corporate visual identity schemes: if a visual device has to be explained, or attached to the company it represents

208

only through exposure and familiarity, this can be an unnecessarily expensive exercise. On the other hand, those schemes which were devised on a whim of the chief executive a hundred years ago can be valuable properties - but only if what they represent has succeeded in spite of them. A shell has nothing whatever to do with petrol nor for that matter does Texaco's star or BP's shield - however, it is unlikely these companies could survive without them.

EMOTION

The sheer emotive power of symbolised identity, from the swastika to the Star of David, from Coca Cola to IBM, is awesome if in the hands of those who understand the mechanics of its manipulation. Consider the 1989 de-Communisation of Eastern Europe; crowds ripping the red star from their national flags - a symbolic act of symbol destruction. The skull and crossbones fluttering above a galleon must have evoked considerable trepidation in those vessels within firing range. In our times, we understand a different meaning when confronted with some product marked with the same device.

Communism abandoned.

The communication power is, however, no less potent. A pierced, initialled heart carved into a tree on some forgotten afternoon must surely give rise to sentiment if encountered at a later date. The same device tattooed on a forearm in a moment of abandon is painfully indelible and probably irrelevant, but nonetheless represents the expression of something

Emotion expressed.

209

The same basic symbol with totally different connotations depending on context.

deeply felt at some specific moment.

Old school ties are worn by those who need the emotional prop of being a part of something tangible and secure. However, to those who recognise their origin, specific characteristics are ascribed to their wearers in advance of any social contact, and in all probability will remain as a preconceived backdrop to any developing relationship.

An established and well organised visual identity can be a powerfully emotive component in our understanding and response to the way in which we see our individual relevance to the world in which we live. A BMW person is different from a Mercedes person although the products are targeted at the same market. A Lacoste T-shirt is aspirational to some, anathema to others. Aggressive people will respond more readily to red than pink.

Emotional response to visual stimuli is one of the platforms on which our society is built, but there is no science of subjectivity. Visual images are created within specific cultural contexts and depend for their effectiveness on the perspicacity and talent of their perpetrators. The corporate identity designer should not simply be a translator of an analyst's conclusions as to the precise nature of market position - rather, he should *add* an informed, subjective and aesthetic dimension to what is, after all, a human connection between reality and perception.

210

THE FUTURE

It is generally true that if one company within a given market decides to represent itself in a light which it considers to be more relevant to that market, its peers will hastily follow suit. Off-licences, airlines and multinationals did it in the seventies, banks, lawyers and retailers in the eighties; the nineties are beginning to see the visual emergence of the socially responsible. Government departments and political parties have started to position their wares, as have charities and trade unions. However, professional bodies are for the most part still saddled with their coats of arms, each one indistinguishable from the next. Universities and polytechnics, because of various imposed restrictions and the need for research finance from industry, will most definitely need to present themselves in a more relevant light. The Church will need to take the leap if it is to survive. Doctors are doubtless soon to raise their practice profiles.

The way in which organisations will in the future express themselves will be controlled by developments in communication technology. Batman-like laser projections of the company logo high in the sky above the corporate headquarters will give an initial profile edge to the pioneers (air traffic control permitting). Holograms will certainly lend depth to the corporate message; miniature flat TV screens might well introduce some life into otherwise dreary business letter headings; annual reports could perhaps be called up on a digital watch.

However our technological environment develops, the visual projection of an organisation's identity and the resultant response will remain dependent on the understanding of its purpose, its culture, its competitors and its markets, and, last but by no means least, the creative skill with which to communicate the essential ethos.

August 1991

Index

214

COMPANIES, CORPORATIONS AND BRANDS

216

217

IDENTITY FACTORS AND COMPONENTS